PROTOTYPE 3

(2021)

CONTENTS

Pavel Büchler & Nick Thurston (4–9)
- *This. For Everyone.*

Ella Frears (10–11)
- Paeon Paean

Sam Buchan-Watts (12–13)
- Listening In

Helen Marten (14–19)
- A tantrum carved from stone

Rachael Allen (20–21)
- from *God Complex*

Rowland Bagnall (22–27)
- Vision of Ezekiel
- Think Fast
- Views of the Winter (November 1899)

Theodoros Chiotis (28–31)
- Deliberate Succession 4–6

Maia Elsner (32–33)
- Still-life
- Replanting

Tom Betteridge (34–37)
- HEURISTIC

Alice Willitts (38–42)
- April is high summer in 2057

Andrew Spragg (43–45)
- from *certain precise instruments, compass me round, or getting to it by gradients*

SJ Fowler (46–48)
- from *Bonobo*

Paul Buck (49–56)
- from *Lies, Lies, and the Rapture of Eden*

Nadia de Vries (57–59)
- Your Hysteria
- Loyalty Test
- Solar Plexus
- Daisy

Maria Sledmere & Frannie Wise (60–63)
- When is the Best Time to Announce a Floral Pregnancy?
- Those Mushroomy Colours

Daniel Kramb (64–68)
- from *Little Estuaries*

Lila Matsumoto (69–71)
- They were amazed at what they saw
- All day the peacocks screamed
- We all know the sound of wine being poured is sleazy

Frances Whorrall-Campbell (72–76)
- Notes from Up High and Down Below

Raluca de Soleil (77)
- *expulsare* (2011–2021)

Olly Todd (78–79)
- Entonox
- Tilia

Stephen Watts (80–84)
- And When I Went …

Natalie Crick (85–86)
- Snow Mam
- Skipping with Julie

Dal Kular (87–88)
- [untitled]
- white pages

Roisin Dunnett (89–91)
- Terrible, Little

James Conor Patterson (92–98)
- LET ME TAKE YOU DOWN 'CAUSE I'M GOING

Karen Whiteson (99–100)
- Runaway Film

Marcus Slease, Calliope Michail & Chris Gutkind (101–113)
- GRAVITY BUBBLES

Ziddy Ibn Sharam (114–117)
- from *The Rubaiyat of Ziddy Ibn Sharam*

Otis Mensah (118)
- The Look

Sam Fuller (119–122)
- from *Raw Ideas*

J L Hall (123)
- Nocturne
- La Laguna Azul

Oliver Sedano-Jones (124–127)
- Birth
- The Ryan Poem

Neha Maqsood (128–129)
- Autumn
- A bitch, a live wire

Antosh Wojcik (130–133)
- The Local Pit
- Yolks

Lauren de Sá Naylor (134–137)
- [untitled]

Astra Papachristodoulou (138–141)
- Apis Tentacular

Eric Langley & James Gaywood (142–147)
- *Pathlines*

Edwina Attlee (148–152)
- January
- February
- March

Campbell Andersen (153–156)
- Spread

Yuri Felsen trans. Bryan Karetnyk (157–162)
- Extras

Contributor Biographies (164–172)

)

POOR

OLD.

TIRED.

Ella Frears

—

Paeon Paean

when we met I
was unruly
overwhipping
undercooking
telling myths of
my inferno
on the ruins
in the bracken
you said nothing
shook the spices
mulled some cider
in a saucepan
I caught fire
in the heatstroke
of your silence
and I burned

(

You were loaf-like
firmest edges
heady scent and
so absorbent
you sopped up my
ego gravy
and you even
asked for seconds
that was when my
sugars softened
hot marshmallow
on a bonfire
panna cotta
set a-jitter
I'm a pitta
puffing steam

when I'm sullen
cooking something
come and find me
in the kitchen
I've been cupping
mozzarella
had my fingers
in the pudding
will you hold me
in the larder
nightshades gleaming
in the corner
will you lift me
like you did that
sack of flour
in the shop

that's enough now
save your bacon
gut the mackerel
cut the lemon
when I walk past
press my body
like you're checking
if I've ripened
set the timer
set the table
mop my clumsy
spilled libations
salt the water
fork a bean to
check it's tender
blow – it's hot

)

Sam Buchan-Watts

—

Listening In

It's apt I'm teased for speaking one language
by a group of refugees who've been displaced
for most of their lives, these boys are puckish
with disbelief, deliberately withholding, I suspect,
their English, or am I paranoid: a fear of
boys in groups, of conspiration, a ball kicked
from nowhere to the back of the head, presides
as I prepare to help teach them about the public
phone box: what it means to make a call
with this antique tech hiding in plain sight,
for a group whose smartphones are a lifeline –
the phone call a useful metaphor
for poetry's one-sided intimacy, the art
an instrument for academic public engagement –
(as I invite the boys in turn to leave a message
on my colleague's answerphone while
their peer group jeers through a door frame
long since retired of glass, exposing them,
rescinding the object's inherent discretion,
the message may be for anyone, I say: living, dead
or otherwise, nobody is listening on the end
of the line, not this time, and that is good,
speak without fear of being misunderstood,
but the boys look more perplexed about where
the money goes than the message or the medium,
who can blame them, so I retain my research
on the booth as embodiment of our interior,
of privacy and confession, national kitsch,
more honest would be to point to universals:
vandalism, caustic stink of piss, I could quote
to them Marshall McLuhan: the booth over-
turns an abstract 'regime of "time" and "space"',
if I did not cringe at the use of 'regime' in this sense,

if I did not fear an inclination to rephrase experience,
to get anxious about how I looked or how
this sounds, how even here I skirt the question
of speaking 'for' in staking common ground.

)

(from *Path Through Wood*)

Helen Marten
—

A tantrum carved from stone
12 loosely traced facets of temper

T¹
A body is equipped with all the material qualities of structure, like a bridge or a building. A figure in X-ray is an image of movement and resistance, gradations of bone and muscle that reveal intensive function, which map and diagram folds or passageways. Pale lilac lines. White ellipses. Scooped bulges of fat: the confrontation between flesh and bone happens around the spine. An X-ray, like a drawing, is a picture of the inherent verb energy of things. Bones are a trapeze for flesh and muscle to climb out into the air, but the very material matter of the skeleton and its articulation means that it is subject to wear and tear. Bones can be broken. The body suffers a very physical kind of hurting. The paradox of strenuous exercise is that it both erodes and strengthens. In mastering movements of the spine, oppositions of quick and slow movements are possible – intensive combinations of immobility and flexibility. Like an animal, the body masters context: it masters the chair and the road; it masters sea and soil; it masters soft and hard. Clothing and houses hold us tight in a friction of fabric. In instances of structural chaos – in accident or rage or illness – the flesh of the body might slip off its bones and become meat.

E²
An egg meanwhile is smooth, a dynamic shell. Unfertilised or raw it is liquid: yolk, albumin, twisted membrane. Dropped on the floor it will almost certainly crack and seep out. Hardboiled with the shell peeled off, the warm white mass of cooked protein is perfectly ovular, dense, throbbing. A small dent at the large end of the curved base is the result of an air pocket, or air cell – the membrane shrinking away from the shell. It is not a chicken or a duck or a bird.

M³
A head taken at collision spills across a road. The world runs around it, a few feet of loose earth fill in the hollows. Time changes and

(

something dark puddles, gurgles a little, foams, reflects the sky,
then dries. Red and blue merge in purple, an ecclesiastical colour,
God in all the details whether you beckon one close or not. A broken
body, a body undone, is a new ruin, something folded in upon itself,
volume lowered. Frank daylight observes. Through the thick rust of a
tree, through the needles and boughs, still there burns a wide blue sky,
almost too lovely to endure.

P⁴
A struck bell reverberates in an infinite number of ways, but only a few
of these cause the surrounding air to vibrate strongly enough to be
audible. The simplest mode gives rise to the lowest frequency vibration
(the lowest pitch); this is called the *fundamental*. All sounds can enter
into the same time structure of music. Time then, is perhaps not
meant as pulse or metronomic speed, but as span or length, and not
something segmented like a ruler, but with the possibility of even and
uneven behaviour, like a tree or a bush, like the weather or the year.
A bell rings with alarm or celebration. A bell bursts like a heart.   )
Old bells are sometimes described as needing to be 're-voiced', a
rotating of the internal mechanised clapper to a different striking point.
Like a head or an egg, then, a bell presents a smooth and curving
surface down which things slip and change.

E⁵
Chronic noise exposure and aggressive behaviour are correlative
variables. The bird that sings an impromptu aria at the break of day
rises through the bloated pinks and purples of morning to rip a new
line of sound on the air, a refrain of mutual peace and exasperation.
Music of all kinds gives us urges – to move, to love, to weep, to die.
It sits deep in the memory of a nervous system bristling with complexity
and stubbornly immovable. Music once heard is always made reanimate
by its resistant foundational qualities, by the sublime effortlessness or
obscenity of having any memory at all. Like speech, it can never be
a singularity.

R[6]
The memory of a single individual, with all its uniquely brilliant hopes and verbal ambiguities, is an enclosed space. A space with virtual noise but not literal noise: the yolk of the brain with its cerebral fluid is, for all its wild business, surprisingly hushed. And we are ashamed of our sounds – our sex, our hunger, our excretions, our taps, our weight, our floorboards. People are curious and exchange lewd grins. Sometimes our own unfulfilled roughness is so abstract as to make us afraid. Singing in the dark is one way to build a wall of sweet sound through which to escape fear. Something like the shoring up of privacies or the fortification achieved by bricks in a garden, all those neat little neighbourhood lines and fences that hem in lawns who lie in pale passivity. The domestic wall serves to phrase a particular kind of familiar space. In the careful enclave of the garden it lends structural meaning to the luminous and refreshing articulations of plants and vulnerable fruits that write out their seasonal scripts and intertwine. Perhaps it also describes the divisional parts of lived equations: on one side all the money and meaning and numerals, on the other side a bog of indeterminate subjectivities.

(

T[7]
Bricks are an intermediary, the needle and thread of architecture. They seep calcium salts that manifest as white chalky streaks across their surfaces, an efflorescence or figurative act of blossoming, much like a flower. After bright sunshine or damp weather or seasons of frugal harvest, small birds clamp onto the mortar and peck the carbonates with delicate exuberance. This dietary boost of calcium is merrily digested, used to form the external shells of their perfect eggs. Sparrows on the stone and birds out in their dozens. Off they go, slitting lines across lakes, immune to the concept of negativity as they break from the water dripping and wild, gargling beaks of algae and simple dirt.

E[8]
The planet wraps its language around multiple dimensions. When birds fly from one overhead electricity wire to another, from roof to scaffolding to billboard, they are tracing a mad grammar in the sky.

They are writing a play. They move through the blues or greys of air like inheritors of an already defined composition. Their presence in any landscape is part of the lyrical contradiction of nature being empirical but full too of allegory. Birds roving in flocks from one patch of sky to another, chapter to chapter, are an exuberantly flourished signature, persistent mutability, lines of ink. Lost birds, left behind birds, damaged birds, are like the stiff graphite of worried pencil over silent paper. A word world, wide and gleaming.

M[9]

Sometimes the optical effect of road and sky is too much for a morning. Those days when we have been too busy inhaling perfume, deodorant, air freshener, windscreen-wiper fluid – when we feel like loose dry skin, stuffed with booze and cheap food as though snipped off some better and fuller person. The circuitry of behaving properly – eating a tidy breakfast, remaining calm – feels humiliating. We feel caught, arraigned for crimes against common chores. A tantrum is like a hurricane. Winds and ocean currents reach singular points of intensity. Multiple processes of air and water swell with wildness, accelerated by temperature or pressure. There is no central command of phenomena, but a set of self-organised movements.

)

P[10]

The primary order of language is found in a newborn infant. A child's cry has few syllables, a howl which rises is not an individual blunting of language, a bleating, but simply part of the aged fact that the sounds a human being learns before expressive speech are the destroyed anterior sounds of distress. Adult feeling is a picture of more nuanced intensities, like a *weatherscape* of experience: rising and fallings of light, sound, colour. Loosening a belt, looking in a mirror, writhing with a lover. At worst, these feelings are a kind of horizontal weather, the barometer neither rising nor falling with great damage, but drifting from side to side. All vertical people are capable of apathy, moving about hugging groceries or lugging books. They crawl through financial or medical instability, through the desperate rage of hunger or bodily dissatisfaction. Bodies get stuffed with melon or steak or shrimp and feel sick on account. Bodies are violently happy. They want to love.

They want to *want* and are riddled with jealousy. Extreme feeling keeps horizontal emotion contained in a vertical shell. Wickedness prospers too, feelings are exposed and furniture broken. Rats prosper. Sparrows and pigeons prosper, surviving with a weed's ease picking meals from the street. Maybe household tensions suddenly burst and leaked blood or tears arrive on a precious rug, a plate is smashed or the cat kicked with no small amount of sincerity. The human head is just as vast and sonic and moving as the Earth. Lots of heads like little planets dropping crumbs. Annoyances add up like shuffled cards, changing values, dividing like elemental organisms. These annoyances fade, but slowly. Irritation is like bad toe fungus – first gone, only to burst out itching and grey when the wrong synthetics are presented, the culprit shoe snuck back into rotation from the rack. Personalities become clowns or prisoners to manage. This is the efficiency of expulsion in a Western city – how readily *matter* of all kinds is trashed.

E[11]
Remorse is a pathology of syntax[1] and nobody *means* to misbehave. Some people smell ground coffee and its sweet nutmeg haze reminds them of home. Of houses in which they grew, tossed small-wheeled bikes without care on lawns or driveways. Homes full of morning appointments and the adult world of protection. Full of coffee, butter, steam. Caffeine might be considered as a national hallucination of fondness and safety. Drunk black and quick, feet sitting like good happy dogs on the floor. In sound terms, the quiet security of the coffee grinder is different to the soft splatter of boiling water. Different to the light and heat of a candle flame, different to the soft blunt shudder of cutting bread, different to the quick slitting determinacy of a sliced lemon. An angry seed burst from a bun is simply relocated to be found in the creases of fabric later, or stuck on a chin because what is matter anyway but always one thing's essence modifying the other – fragrance, size, *feeling*? And then like the crass machines we are, there comes the biting, the chewing, swallowing emulsifying, absorbing, shitting.

R[1]

Still the birds arc and dive. Big stones are moved and small stones are moved, and ideas feel like tiny drops of wine in a groaning wide ocean. Pain fills a pillow and is put to bed. The road thickens and car tyres slow to a stop, as if spun with syrup in afternoon's boiling tilt. On one side of the planet the rain continues: waters bury deep and herbs rise, tomatoes rise, salad in dark and wild shapes bloom fervent greenness. On the other side of the planet, the sun slits everything to sticks and plankton blooms first with erotic mania then dies. Stems rot and the forest is full of hormones. Every disease is considered as requiring a specific remedy: chemicals, solvents, bed rest, favourable soil and limestone gravel. The rhythmic machinery of nature, with all its cogs and sewers and recycling systems, is more finessed and beautiful than any body might manage to be. All things can be like hieroglyphs inhabited and treasured by those who have discovered the symbolism of each of them. Whole communities feel calm or civilised by their proximity. The price of famine. The price of dancing. The price of loving. All the numbers are hung up in windows on the street. Found money feels far more monetary than the coins scraped from one's own purse. In amongst it all, long figures move out of shadows. Between coughing, between kitchen vanilla and pancakes, between riverbeds dried up, weather exerts itself and marks its lines, its noises. Perhaps some stalks come later – happy lines, some green – and then Marigolds poke up in the North and the Roses rear in the South. There is evidence of change.

)

—

[1] J.H. Prynne, from 'Of Movement Towards a Natural Place'

Rachael Allen

—

from *God Complex*

(

I have a chaotic
element, it
connects me
to the ground.
Green stamp
round sky
peach lidded
grey effort
of collusion
shoulder of
nebular blue
sky touching
crouched over
or slouching
the way
machinery does
democratic
and still
on a Sunday.
How to cart off
such deep pain?
I look up
for company
at the sheet-
white sky
with medicinal blues
or to where
a barren tree
fluorescent
reaches up
like a woman
and the iridescence
of a smell
like old meat
on thermals
thin stink
on the air
an animal
scent glimpsed
unspeakable things
happen everywhere
discontent
is rice-white
and clogged
like you
who are
lilac with cold

In my head
 time works
  on a flattened
   disk. I look out
   through stained
   glass, a window
feeling, touching
 my head and neck   )
  for religious
   lumps, I'm not sure
  but I might
have a deity in me –

 lucid angel in
  the soft glass –

Rowland Bagnall

—

Vision of Ezekiel

The sky is patching.
Outside the clouds
are doing that *are we
secretly smoke* thing
they sometimes do
Their specific meanings
heavy-laden,
obviously full of weight

the frail sun
feels good and nice
just-now mounting the
horizon
in every century
(an outrageously
beautiful mountainous
view

whose shape is yet to
be determined
What else was there?
teenage bathers
unimpressed by the
spectacle
the crowd making its
way back down

And what to do about
the new haze of
crispness
retooling
this part of the plain,
an unstable mixture

of things as they are
all of the time

whatever that means
for you.
Imagine, as you're
forced to in this scene,
the unevenly
distributed weight of
the present
A familiar door

pointing out how
language stretches over
something it can't
quite cover
overwhelmed by detail
announcing itself
into the speaker's
mouth, not with an 'I'

)

but an 'us'.
It feels dark blue
I feel like if I close my
eyes I'll see
a group of future-
holding
days
not yet embarked upon

submarining
with the promise of
anticipation
which also reminds
me of various scenes
in Lean's *Doctor
Zhivago* (1965).
and the snow, it keeps

coming back across all of these,
a kind of shorthand for experience.
it 'spreads' you.
it has many lives.
how else would anybody ever notice

the deep-ice connection between things described [and] other things?
the splendour of meaning
bleeding out of them at every turn

(

Think Fast

Light filters in.
There is a tightness in the dusk, like love.
The day evolves beyond your need for it.
So, tell me, are you

feeling seen?

        α

The rain outnumbers us.
No sign of it stopping through these hours
of unglistened night. Nothing to do but to give
yourself over. Marvel at the

squeegee dawn.

        α

Same problem, same solution.
The solid-seeming water holds the mountains
like a cradled face. Drag your deer to the roadside,
splattered with headlights.

Any questions?

        α

Coffee and apple juice
out on the deck. I watch the shadows leeching
colour from the bracken and the fleeting dew.
Pray, how do you

enlanguage that?

        α

Fade out autumn.
Bring in winter's sleek returns.
A friend wipes ash from the hood of her car.
Horizons razorblade

to view.

α

What does your suspicion say?
Freezing waters. Mulching leaves. A sun
-bronzed cafeteria. The morning scoops light
on the sand. Nobody sees.

Go figure.

α

The meagre light remembers you,
touching up your skin-gloved hand. The weather mirrors
yesterday's. Simple and uncomplicated. Enjoy it, Pal,
while you still can. Let day's train

overrail you.

α

Total yellow. Screens of trees.
I sit at the window, through which I see
other things. I watch for them, I listen out,
and that is

the situation.

α

Funny thing is, you give it
shape and – giving shape – a meaning.
The brief reign of the frost is done.
Is it really

any wonder?

α

At last, the thick-skulled hours
retreat. What's in it for them, anyhow? The sun crowns
lightly into view, a silent transmission, and the feeling comes to you
like warmth or like an almost abstract kind

of pain.

Views of the Winter (November 1899)
　for AH

I

because it is winter,
because the yellow afternoon is short,
because the grass can't move as it wants to,
because the crowds around the pool have stopped,
because you can still feel the night's residual cool in the earth,
because the dirt hems their cloaks,
because it has happened,
because it is happening,
because the light skims at the edge of things,
because the new wet low sky pinks,
because the water petitions you, calling you out,
because the darkness wants to know where you go each day,
because the colours break their surfaces,
because this scheme of things is fixed,　　　　　　　　　　　　　　　　　　　　　　　)

I

because it is winter,
because it strips the park in sheets,
because the people are strolling, controlling the atmosphere,
because the trees are shielding trees,
because you have a thought and feel it,
because your inattention jolts,
because the water is one way and sun is another,
because it punctuates the earth,
because this all takes up its place again a century ahead of you,
because the upper branches merge,
because if you think about it nothing that much has changed,
because you see it seeing you,
because it is happening,
because it stands to happen soon,

Theodoros Chiotis

—

Deliberate Succession 4–6

(

Theodoros Chiotis

(

These visual poems belong to a larger sequence depicting the mythical figure of Geryon at the time of his death. The sequence investigates both the hybrid nature of the giant as well as the multiple ways in which we experience time. As such, these pieces layer a series of three elements referencing the three bodies and the three heads of Geryon and the triplicate nature of time (past-present-future):

- The bottom layer is a poem in English about Geryon's bodies subsequently translated into binary code and turned into an image.
- The middle layer is the Geryon poem translated into modern and classical Greek. The translations were turned into images that were cut up and rearranged in reverse order over the binary code.
- Finally, the text of the poem was cross-referenced with Apollodorus 2.4.1–4 and Hesiod, *Shield of Hercules*, 223–4, and select passages were superimposed over the text.

)

Maia Elsner

—

Still-life

in photographs. Plotted on the X axis,
time. What is left of it. The vertical

is a ladder to a slide. You throw me up,
catch me as I come down. Later,

at the kiln, you show me a clay-growth.
The root of a new city. You & I mix

soil. Red for the bleeding town, brown
for the buried bank. How God made

us. Raw & open. There is no home-
land, just the skip in which we tip

(

this cracked surface. Try again. Each
night we mislay ourselves. Mistake

the moon for whole. Dig the ground
for dandelion heads. Decapitated stalks

like soldiers stand. Each day they know
too much. Your breath is harder now.

Your skin, purpling. Less ink to mix,
your strokes like words, are frail

decisive. I will remember this. How
wax lights gold into your cheeks.

Replanting

strands like lives   budding
                               ash children
the morning loosens
                  limbs
                      replay

a damp living room   ransacked
                           in watercolour
       petals like faces
                 crumpled so

paint them   back to light
                         ochre as day
as each day invents
                two minutes
                & nineteen seconds
more   )

than what existed
                yesterday   watch the sun

                    hold on as if for breath
the edge-pull ever stronger, pause

           at the brink   say yes

as a coal tit flashes   between traffic lights

Tom Betteridge
—
HEURISTIC
    after Éliane Radigue and Rhodri Davies

(

delicate
in gain in-
delible
resonance
ingrows
in string
abrasion
grains up
in ease
and curls
against
spindle
branch of
dwindling oak
lone rust-
leaf
suspense
in glasswork's
extension
into
curvature
reddens
and clots
shot dead
what I was
to float
free transit of growing-pink
lint through frosts
restrung
disclosive
nautic
from silo

clothwork two
bows
across harp
sigh
siphon
clot-tickle
procession
pinned in cove
frit-weight
bins
default mode network
every
note
collapses in form under
glisten-
stress
becomes over-
tone
formation   )
that clothes
branch
now also a clot
posset
sharded
dragged
back though reddening
clout-
time
unfurler
to lower in blanket space
across
and through
vibration
starts
moro reflex
splays out limbs
lith-

Tom Betteridge

bellows
affixed
seizure
sore clot
strings
infant mobile
red
clothed
leaves shudder
alacrity
acrid hanging cloth-
breath
solid lung
matter
plug-hair
spun nervous
loss
compression
(try again to understand what a father is
terror
branched ice forms
in raised bed bleed-out
stolid parsnip
root tendril
dampened
soil-warmth
at skin-threshold
cut into
form
to be held by
who first
up to strip light
strict air and latex
expelling default
world
from lung
inhaling

worlds' curling
sound warps
in egress
beaded
influence clots on
string harsh with parabola
ice extention
along clot-branch
tripped
re-
breath expulsion
summoning
relation into up-
breath down-
breath

)

Alice Willitts

—

April is high summer in 2057

i. the new seashore in Cambridge; a closed door

lost children hooded eyes a dust
kicking geography in circles
beating my womb so rounded
on a generation I lean on seasoned
woodgrain ash maybe I count our
migrating footfalls in a kind of patience
travel on the smell a salty flood has
seeping back into my garden I miss
the simple hyacinth
pungent hippopotamus of flowers
friend a voice says *very little*
that is real just vanishes when it dies
(no Alice you're wrong
remember how heaviness could
be dug from mud at Barrington
held in museums or hands
the riven sea will be scouring now
bones are selfless in two ways
they're drowned again there's a song
I know about love its house is plain
the ground is steady the door open
but from the window the Cam laps up
new waves dragging the poplars
still hustling a convincing river-
tongue along the bank we stood on
swam off before we drifted in a clear
past charmed by your murmuring
earth — heart I said rock belly
head you said leaf hand — cloud
fleshed words quarrelling on & on

ii. there is the territorial blackbird; heat leaving the day; Jorie Graham, Alice Notley & Alice Willitts sit round the kitchen table in Hertford Street

we are stitching light to the wall. marking the year's days
    by their heat. a pattern of place
the plaster holds in seams. creasing behind our needles
    like sear-sucker.

we stitch. regular work. in. out. dashes accumulate.
    murmuring stitches. slant
to where we were born. our landscapes or were they
    cities? winter. a small room. essential. heat.
has fire ever not sung? our songs. carry the sacred
    even though we are not all believers.
we task ourselves to carry it home
    like birds sing themselves out & back. daily

when women were birds. sometime ago now. cracking   )
    ice-time & freeing squawks. our vowels were
birthed on hilltop places. our wings took moonlight
    smoothing vanes into blood in return for arms.
& isn't the feminine all arms anyway. how many times
    do we want to fly away? lifting our arms.
we hold the origins. you can starve love
    by binding women's arms.

chain link & running. we stitch. regular work. say
    we kill the children. yes. with each birth we kill.
aggression towards our kind is the first war.
    we are not killers. o not en masse. but still. regularly.
we carry baby. we feed baby. we hold baby. we grow
    baby. to kill another baby. stitching
our running voices our cloths for blood.
    monthly. giving directions.

Alice Willitts

shall we time the heavy flight of the bee
    or the fern fronds. their mass uncurls day.
when we look out over green green we're moved
    without being transported. say time
is flying when missiles traject a foreign border.
    man's grasp of time is the tracer glow of stealth.
we only name impact. 'Storm Shadow'
    strikes. night closes on our voices.

tomorrow we three. at my kitchen table on Hertford St
    hunting for stories in seams. faces
can cry with other faces. we can. & do not
    mistake us for sentimental.
the blackbird knows its astonishing
    awl of sound. i nest fears in my mind.
& in my body. the baby stretches. plants a foot
    on my rib. forward rolls. onto my cervix.

(while in your mind the clock goes ahead
    still. we are all patterns with other patterns.
a singular material woven from finest loops of time
    we stitch. to see ourselves made.
now i make tea & baby settles as i move around.
    rinse the pot. i want to tell you how *i think like tea*
sometimes floating. the baby as me.
    breathing

in a sympathetic mitochondria. baby & me.
    breathe. the way nerves through flesh
make an intricate organ. voices lick along
    our hyphatic threads. soothing us. breathe.
in rhyming ions. set water to boil.
    a free movement. breathe. survive. twist cloths
round the hot cups for handles. at the table
    we wait. we sew. tea. baby. in me.

iii. here are raw materials

                your tiny arms fly outwards   surprised

by the vastness of your reach   we all travel out

where we came in   at least once   to make this turning

& taste the first fungal mouth in a rush of fluid

slowed mucosal priming   ears rinsed of the heartbeat   fingers

in the touch of the other   a nose for air & a milk

mouth   skin to skin in your metallic scent   sweet

i am glued to this first marvel   like a drop of time   )

is hurtling from me to all the furthest places

right up close

         life's weave loops us   the pattern-making

animal   did image & sound start together

with the first cry? the first face?   us   cut

you & i were one fabric

& now?   a seam

feeds you   how i'm already sewing you into place

even as the ruin of placenta follows you out

Alice Willitts

    the space of my arms

               filled with your beauty is scarce

    & looking back at me

    such that carrying you

    i'm naked

        the sea has come to our door   naming us

      child   mother

    such a familiar sound & soil

    still   too soon for sand

    though if i tell you these things

(it is to sew them into new cloth

    chain & running   my feet nudge

    the waves of the muddy shore   i'm looking out

    at alders & willows

    i thought you would climb

    submerged

            bare crowns

    making me peculiar company

Andrew Spragg

—

**from *certain precise instruments, compass me round,
or getting to it by gradients***

XIV II

A special note from our friend – our more missed
forever – 'don't let ourselves settle to
see what has come. I dance around the sense
of it, and loosened to a sputter, light
moves in swift patches, and then has gone. Get on
this fragrant behaviour, best foraged in
between mouthfuls of posh French butter, let
the gills sing out, grayish in colour –'
hiccup, '– in faith we restore heaven's flight
and say there slugger, what star better than
this one then or this one forever, eh,
so vain a prospect, then so vain the field.   )

The cattle glowered, men fell asleep, sun
came shuffling, I will say no more than –'

XIV I

He said success is there inside of you –
a round incline – hostile as that presents.
And I suspicious of this behaviour
often enforced, rarely with flourish;
you, sickening to the season, say what
about it – stay with my book, stay with my
weather and forever is appetite
unconnected. A little tranche, less shape
after a spell, and much of it made more
to its detriment, all shuffle, no flair.

It is then you try convince you yourself
you are long out of it, something to bind,
a hunger, teeth and shadow, and neither
a foe or friendless. So I drank too much.

(

XIV III

it is spent autumn sun and seen breaching
horizon, blue it strengthens then and then,

but that it seemed shallow in all forms,
gathering pace in pools, the summer we

all gradually forgot. Finding it then
and, listen, where you sounded all livid

this morning in finding it bolshily
presented. You, this heart in a bucket.

And there is no place where we can think more
clearly, it rounds onto our placid footsteps.

Then these unjust and seeming feelings that
fall on top of such other feelings –   )

it's become too frustrating to measure.
I find myself in an unreliable mind.

SJ Fowler

—

from *Bonobo*

a flea favours the same areas

as a lover

here is a book maker for heretics

one can hardly imagine in what diversity

an ape can develop their debaucheries

all they need is a permissive partner in crimes who can set down in detail those things

when the imagination ape is inflamed, however great is variety

in all other passions, it is greater here, the abberations of this way

shall we distinction between that which is imagined and that is done?

(

nah, they can be the same in VR and if you try hard enough

sober science catalogues text us into perversions too

we had a good time didn't we?

fastidious in the bathroom, dirty in the bedroom? welcome to town

we had a good run did we not

oi toad nimbus

oi rubicon rose

oi hunger child

oi ribbon oven

oi effect and cause

oi cork eyes

oi gas mask

oi glue stick

don't pretend to Bonobo

bo's on time

bon's not acceptable stereotypes

bono's with your daughter she's fine having fun even

bonob's hangs your head in ignomy

bonobo's a circular artery

or a square field

or in denial

Bonobo is not your pathetic girlfriend boyfriend

Bonobo is not your excuse

Bonobo is not simplicity for the limited capacity

Bonobo is mysterious blanket of wanting to do things   )

Bonobo is Cordelia before all the bother

Bonobo attains the sea bomb wetness of your root

it is 1488 and cardinal is sniffing the arse

of his dog

o clement supermother

and it is 1677 and the marquis de sade is writing

what you thinking

because he is an ape aristocrat shaved just right

to get in history

and bonobo is reading this and thinking I am tame

compared to homosap ingenuity

and bonobo is rereading this and getting erect

while columns are being written about microhappenings

his Bonobo is being

grown up

and babies and other catastrophes

and the perversions next door, the wanking at the desk

and desire for a throat to be gabbed

and a face to be lapped

while the columns like line letters that say

how could the slapping?

(

Paul Buck
—
from *Lies, Lies, and the Rapture of Eden*

The hungry savages barged through **the door to the war cabinet**. The table was bare. Straw-Cogs tripped Stick-Stove, who fell and dented his forehead on the mahogany table.
Remember your place,
Straw-Cogs reminded the turps-smelling turncoat who was boss, boot stamped on his groins. Short-Tricks marched in slamming the steel door back into the wall. Plaster crumbled. He instructed everyone to their places, then shuffled the pus-stained place cards around. The assembled shifted chairs. He barked orders to start, walked out, monitoring their blubbers would proceed from central command as he worked at other notches in his strategy.
Fuck them all,
was the first pronouncement that purpled the air. Square-Jaw needed a shit. A bucket was propped in the corner. Best on offer.
Not plastic,
enunciated a smirking voice, owner not discerned.
Thought that was a sick bucket,
Hand-Job spluttered, raking a rusty key up and down his arm, looking for a vein to irritate and explore, gouge.

The slugs living in the wall crevices, **waiting for the sperm to spill**,
we're ordering,
the servers had been copulating and had no time to clean themselves. Flies still remained gaping. Pictures of degeneration excited Rotary-Blade, painted lips and long varnished fingernails and the sharpened ends of the crosses dangling on their bare chests. Churlish probably, but where were the dollops of mustard?
I breathe the armpits.
One opened his fly further and breathed anew. In the furnace of an outward relishing, the pain of Rotary-Blade

was succoured. He bit off the end of one of his dildoes. He wanted better. The vibrancy of undulating hips and slapped thighs was a mouthful for Rotary-Blade. Bank-Rout swayed over, shrugging off all help with a wave of his bared knife. This is what greeted everyone each time.

You come back to basics,

the meatballs. The fragrancy of the open flies was enough to seduce him too. Little by little they were reeled in. He would be amazed if he survived the afternoon. Later, when they reached the room in the city where his family had kept a secluded hideaway, he rolled back the carpet. There was a painting spread on the floor that had him trembling wildly. The bedroom had similar images, all phallic, all derived from the knicker-twisters, Félicien Rops and George Grosz. They whimpered and imagined that the art of walking across phalluses was like a religious ceremony for people of their breeding. Rotary-Blade was full of bombast and baked transgressions. While Bank-Rout smoked he spread wide his buttocks and looked around for a door knob. Grinning afterwards,

there's a younger brother at home.

The bunny outfit suited Rotary-Blade.

You don't know what will be rent.

And a narcissistic breath emerged from his elevated lips, accompanied by his habit of pulling images of puckered lips from his pockets. Bank-Rout made a point of ignoring them, dazed but eyeing the bruised thighs. The genius of his actions was to surround himself with city boys, and for the dilapidated commissioners to ride high.

We hire a taxi,

the first lad sprawled on the sofa suggested, dangling another carrot.

We can see what your sights are set on,

and he signalled for his phone.

We use subtlety.

And another lad burst his sides laughing, spewing cocktails across the upholstery. The unshaven were driven beneath, hunched over mobile phones that had long since become redundant. All relevant contact was made by burners. Orders were made verbally, committing to the written word was verbotten. Once written, it was more difficult to be denied. Fluidity was the means by which power subsisted.

They entered the treasury office, **women in dresses** out to lose control of themselves. Suits flirted and an actor delivered his lines, considering himself as prime beef.

Anyone who doesn't play ball, release their personal details and addresses.

Instructions delivered, taped extracts of how often Short-Tricks had driven a bus over those who failed were played. A man who murders in order to survive.

A crash landing to keep their bodies from pedestrians staging echoes.

Though the thought had been agreeable, in order to soften the silk costumes,

to think that there is a spot where all ideas could be left,

Grain-Monkey addressed Hail-Tooth,   )

a confluence of cock-ups is how we govern,

recalling how Short-Tricks used to sit in his car outside homes where those who threatened his position stepped out to their fate.

Who was holding that damned timeless clock?

All the same, to see that dread and claustrophobia,

oh yes, these things are truly jagged, a compulsion.

Grail-Monkey pulled tight on her bodice, her leggings running with tears, the end of a journey that would

tonight

become what could be indulged in, guilty revelations, stabbing gestures that always made him think of bars where women are reassuring in these matters.

You are here.

The pieces of broken mirror reflected their damaged dreams.

I know you well.

Only Rotary-Blade could violate his victims as a cast. Perhaps he was only a counterfeit of his predecessor. Rotary-Blade had become hysterical, and quietly led away to his ruin.

It is not too hot in the oven? Surely you can bathe in the madhouse.

To recite policies as poems, to reveal a cruel detachment which wandered in, slipped into a stale and abandoned glass of Chabril that belonged with his ledgers. Hanging their heads low, the matter of discussions collapsed them, tittered with them and the inevitable disappearance,

legged it.

If they were able to prevent that burst, that petulant witness who might be made to find it harder to hear voices,

while you are here,

she had never moistened and survived tightening over the inevitability and entirety of Rotary-Blade's death. Hail-Tooth performed abuses that were cruder, screamed into the sheets that nothing more than pouting underlips and soothings were to be heaped in the chamber. A firm hand, the very one with which she had found the dynamics. How useless was the belt, or the whip, rejected in her lap. They had been relevant once. She had been relevant once. They had been together, like two enormous cheeks back to back.

(

Short-Tricks was not to be found in his office, he was **milling about in the network** of corridors and bunkers beneath ground level where ministers retreated to avoid the torrents of abuse and bric-a-bracs thrown, bouncing against the emergency shutters erected throughout Whitehole.

No buts, or ifs... no leakages. Watertight,

had belched through the tannoy system every hour. Bank-Rout cornered Short-Tricks in the toilet releasing his bowels.

Nothing half-baked. Watertight. Are you dumb? Don't you understand orders? And tell them, always tell them, no one, always, no one is available.

Farmers had been marking animals for the chop, as councils had done for weeks with trees being readied for fuel shortages.

You sound as incompetent as those barking through megaphones.

His annoyance at shouting at the metal door caused further explosions into the porcelain.

Man up, you fucking wimp.

It was all hot air. Bank-Rout had fled, his wife would feel the wrong end of the stick, if he was ever released that night. If he could find her. She was holed up in a friend's home, their mews *pied-à-terre* blocked by police against the rioting peasants.

The rust from Short-Trick's hands shifted **onto the bodice of the undulating** and hesitating Floor-Lick, begging him for a more agreeable spot for her next appearance at the cabinet session.
You mean you are going to deliver me, passed up, despite my clumsiness?
She had spewed bile on the carpet, her frivolous game-plan, her ruggedly elemental insight into how to handle and explore the cool white skin of Fixed-Grin, her lithe and delicate contours... The next moment there was a grating commotion and Dump-Fling pushed her way into the office, wearing little more than a flimsy curtain with a huge Byzantine cross that bounced against her breasts. She had pumped seventeen bullets into the body of her aide before they had stopped her trigger-happy finger from its vibrating spasms. There were sounds of pain rising and falling from behind her, though her approach had beckoned others to prostrate themselves and beg for her attention. Her spittle was sliding into a new and moving direction, fragments of tumultuous applause and shouts of acclamation came together.
I can smell her breath,
intoxicated by caresses, she was revealed as Stick-Stove's vassal when the less than contented sounds of another disagreeable minister pouring scorn might reach the point of discouragement.
I had only to think neutral and *you must get away and begin a new life.*
Her grace and her abrupt gestures were totally unexpected.
Does that mean you don't love me anymore?
asked Short-Tricks.
Fuck off.
The first-time assistant, emboldened by his tourist diploma, was even now more adept than she would ever be. She did not

know who he was, but he was a threat, glaring eyes, dribbling juices on his chin.

Fuck you too. Swing from trees.

Her stance had been singled out ever since her first day in the post, before the department sank beneath her stilettos, grimacing and wobbling and ready to run riot.

A woman can inflict power on a wimp like you

and she produced a rod, ran it up his left thigh. It was already dripping with sweat. His buttocks were bared, oozed excitement. The cushion on the couch was withdrawn and she brushed her long hair across the seat to sprinkle the dust from the mercury potion. She was dry and less than regal. But her thighs were becoming damp.

There was a **part-blown inflatable doll** seated in the corner. Caught out, Straw-Cogs sidled across and sat forcefully, hoping to make it bang. He was rewarded by a low and long farting sound as the plastic deflated with a show of defiance. Hand-Job rushed forward, suggested a doctor be called. Pickled-Pox disappeared after a few moments, never to return. His chair was filled by Bomb-Slack, who reacted agitatedly to the cushion fixed to his seat, filled as it was with ball bearings. Block-Lock grinned. It was fully deserved. He had little time for his colleague after he found him urinating against his office door. He had embarrassed him by sending out his secretary, who was then drenched in the flow of piss.

We're not eager to fight this war on legal terms.

Action and whatever energy were needed would be wasted. A sense of defence against a counter-attack had never been so absolutely mastered. Into war without resistance was the creed. Hail-Tooth felt the rest of her flesh burning.

War.

The question was she had barely done anything right, although she was still there fighting because Tongue-Stirrup vouched for her. She lost with every bet she made, every option always fell on deaf underwear.

England is finished. You mean Scotland. Yes, Scotland is finished.

When her business ventures had sacrificed lives, the sole option was to kill off the witnesses to her dubious dealings. Alone. She had been ushered out the back, locked in a cupboard. She was still talking.

I had glimpses...

She would be shot if she escaped, her tongue was too loose.

Remove an eye,

Short-Tricks demanded. For the moment no one moved.

I was reminded, piddle piddle...

And it was only due to his skill at not being skilful that he was able to stop the proceedings. Straw-Cogs slipped into a leather pair of shorts and went out back to the cupboard in search of another inflatable.

Straw-Cogs imitated **the behaviour of a Roman** emperor, stealing out at night, dishevelled and in disguise, appearing in any area of his choosing, for all the underground passages were open to him, to be exploited and explored in whatever way he could fathom. He was famed for his behaviour of assaulting young women and stealing from the poor and defenceless, just for the sheer hell of it. The bravado vibrating through him revealed that dreams would not hide, that they would make the point clear. Always had done.

But she was your neighbour.

A black suit and he was stroking the vicious-looking feline. Desire for his partner's friend was inconsequential. He snatched up a soiled towel as soon as the sweat was absorbed. Sexual desire was in his hair. After a while, the new pick-up began to want recognition for herself, in the same way her name was shaken from her hair. He pulled the cape more tightly. He was there to represent a sense of loss, couches piled high with pillows and lights that could lean towards a meaning of the particular. And she did nothing to correct what she knew to be wrong.

Your lusts are mostly dreams.

That was not an expression he allowed to be heard. Momentary despair spanned the truth into lies. The table was shaking, her head banged hard against the top as he tried to console his desires. He kept his thighs apart and directed his father to coax his penis to its favourite port of call, for he had no feeling of having a body, just power.

(

Nadia de Vries

—

Your Hysteria

stumbles into success and loses
her sympathy directly after.
Like leprosy we shun our friends' success.
Your hysteria is not here to make friends.
Your hysteria likes to go on solitary walks
Your hysteria has no menarche and no end.
Your hysteria luxuriates in long blue coats
in the dead of every winter.
Like winter, women immortalise themselves
by dying once a year.
Like women, your hysteria is complex –
you wouldn't understand!
Beige is the least charismatic colour;
your hysteria hates it.
She won't face the winter cold in it,
let alone the pleasantry of summer.
Your hysteria has no horoscope.
Your hysteria dates German doctors.
Your hysteria likes dogs and walks on the beach.
Life is not a beach.
Your hysteria hates it.

Loyalty Test

The key to raising dogs is to praise them when they're good
and to punish them when they're bad.

If you raise them successfully,
you will be rewarded with endless
loyalty, loyalty, loyalty.

If you raise them unsuccessfully,
they will bite you in the face and,
depending on the size of the dog,
you might require stitches.

(**Solar Plexus**

I ground myself
I perform myself
I reprimand my inner child

Daisy

The chicken is taken from the coop.
The chicken is placed upon the chopping block.
The chicken's head is removed.
The chicken's bowels are emptied.
The chicken's feet are removed.
The chicken is submerged in water.
The chicken is plucked with precise and routine-like movements.
The chicken is sent to a different room.
The chicken is roasted to a crisp.
The chicken is bought by a human family.
The chicken is eaten.
The chicken disappears.

)

Maria Sledmere & Frannie Wise

—

When is the Best Time to Announce a Floral Pregnancy?

A cube of dandelions
weep in the open field, a lily in my belly.
Do you remove a single bloom?
Mother-in-law comes by in her customary
pollen to call them weeds
which reminds you sneezingly of a childhood incident
concerning the lovely clover brought home
in bundles
like 'mum I made us a lucky bouquet!'
but anything might have been trash
and crushed from suspicion
daughterly after

All the wild dandelions turn
(towards different suns is a wild explanation

Had I plucked each one
the way you look at four o'clock
and turned complex ache
with only the beautiful stems
of your naming
worried a floret this all would collapse
miles ago in chamomile loneliness
everything closes to sleep
every part useful:

A catalogue of white-flowering Japanese dandelion,
endangered Californian dandelion, northern dandelion,
Turkish dandelion, Russian dandelion
which produces rubber, red-seeded dandelion,
Korean dandelion, common dandelion
found in many forms, the rare dandelion of St Kilda
will I ever go there?

Endemic to the area is also insomnia

Having assembled for you this sculpture
weeping milky latex, vomit-
a-thought, called up
lion's-tooth care or piss-a-bed yellows;
every year Americans spend millions
on lawn pesticides to have uniform lawns
of non-native grasses
an effort which uses 30% of the water supply

Here are some useful facts.

Those Mushroomy Colours

I swore the Pleiades were watching
Us step over the carmine blots
And our larchy mothers
In the loam and fallows,
The swallows

Here we were fettered in the boughs
I brought so much of longing
Cowed and cloven; we'd belonged to the land
That stood and watched us ripen
As we wept deciduous sluice
Beneath the sessile
Poised to cradle
You had looked so revolted

At how they fell from me
In sweet incorrigible loops
Laurel; my wretched fastes
I put you down first
To pluck the oranges and lemons
Push the husks around my mouth in
Blood moons and juicy little suns
I would baste my tongue
With such sweetness
And call it gossamer

In those mushroomy colours
When fingers became such
Peachy arcs that blushed and
Pushed at that pastoral braille
This liquid feeling
I haul it up to my chest
Let me sleep in this sundry maypole
With my duvet full of ribbons

(from *Notes Towards an Orange Fish*)

Daniel Kramb
—
from *Little Estuaries*

        Where light swims,
        slowly, to a some-
        where:

(Your
        mind re-
        thinks its territory

Washing, towards
bare feet, as
words:

You know   )
there is no staying
here. You cannot hear translation.

Daniel Kramb

From alcoves, imagined,
low at
night:

(Swept,
skeletons
of a singing

Clouds cracked. A low
light shim-
mer:

Strength   )
like a gust
in your bones

Daniel Kramb

Hands up against
the sky, you
sculpt:

(Tide-
taken.
Its cannot swim

Lila Matsumoto

—

They were amazed at what they saw

They were amazed at what they saw… a huge self-portrait of the artist, dressed like a general, sitting proud on a mound of voluptuous cushions. Next to it was a work that really made them gasp. A work that had never been seen before, having been locked away in the temperature-controlled vault of the eremitic, now-deceased, patron-of-the arts. The painting was done in the characteristic style, impasto to the point of pastry. The usual mountains and rushing streams. But when they looked more carefully, a hidden landscape emerged in the dizzying folds of ultramarine. There were two brocaded bays retreating, a tender mummy. A mendicant carrying a fresh sense of loss whipped up in tempera. And a doorknob wearing a ruff, signalling the rudderless drift of life. The world is all here, they thought.

)

All day the peacocks screamed

All day the peacocks screamed outside the building where the conference was taking place. In one panel, three men spoke with authority about a venerable literary figure. In another panel attendants watched a clip of gorillas performing a waterfall ritual. Lunch was taken on the lawn in the presence of the peacocks dragging their tail feathers, mewling from the parapets, shitting. In the afternoon plenary, attendants were instructed to form groups of three, and to take turns walking slowly around the room with eyes closed, while the other members of their group performed three actions on their bodies: swipe, pat, and jiggle. Later the conference organiser's car was found being scratched up by a peacock which had seen its own reflection in the bonnet.

(

We all know the sound of wine being poured is sleazy

We all know the sound of wine being poured is sleazy, each propulsion of liquid galloping eagerly, even cheesily, into the glass. Don't get me wrong – I'm not parched to the promise of effervescence. These were the things most commonly brought to the party: keys so large you rest them on your shoulder, fragrant boxes, small black books which no one ever seemed to open. Riveting, too, were the guests' lineaments. Such gorgeous crimson pile and velvet silks, arranged in ogeed arches. Here a cambric surcoat, there a resplendent skirt trailing to the ground, garnished with infinitesimal crystal berries. And there were at least four people with wings strapped to their backs. They parroted each other, barefoot, their toes in extreme angles, so mysterious in their attitudes. No doubt they had conferred as to the arrangement of their compositions.

)

(from *Two Twin Pipes Sprout Water*)

Frances Whorrall-Campbell
—

Notes from Up High and Down Below
   a libretto for Chris Burden's *220*

[to be sung in any order by four people stood on fourteen-foot ladders above twelve inches of electrified water]

I.
I work in a seafood restaurant.
I spend all morning with my hands
in a bucket preparing fish.
Cleaning and gutting while the
sand falls into the bucket,
enough to make a sandcastle at
the beach.
Pearls form when an irritant
enters the shell of an oyster, a
muscle, or a clam
Not a grain of sand, but a
parasite, covered in layers of nacre
enrobed in this iridescent shell.
I once dreamt a grain of sand fell
into my eye.

II.
When he was six my son loved to
climb trees in our garden.
Big apple trees at the bottom of
the hill. Five in total, gathered in
a circle.
Their blossom was so sweet, I can
still smell it now.
One day, my son, he fell from
the tallest.
Only about the height of my
husband, but for a six-year-old.
Luckily his jeans got caught in the
branches and broke his fall.
But that winter, my husband took
an axe and cut down all the trees.
He was so angry that I'd let our
only child go up them.

III.
Tomorrow my sister is driving
down from New York to see me.
Our brother was killed in a
motorcycle accident.
He was going too fast and
skidded into a streetlight.
His body looked so fragile in
the morgue.
We are going to scatter his ashes in
the fields near where we grew up.
On the day he died I was coming
home from work.
When I stopped at the
intersection, someone had hung a
pair of shoes over the cables.
They dangled leg-less in the great
blue sky.

IV.

I am reading a book where
people are turned into trees.
Their human bodies are then
flung across the branches, their
skin torn by the thorns — oh it
is a horrible image.

V.

Today we went walking in the
fields by our house.
The sun was out and it was
warmer than we had expected —
I had to take my jacket off.
I hung it on a tree whilst we
went for a swim.
Ever since I got married I have
had nothing to do.
Luke takes care of me so well.

VI.

A homeless man has taken to
sleeping outside my apartment.
When I left this morning he was
curled in the porch like a cat.
I had to step over him.
His milky white eyes stared up at
me like coins in the bottom of a
fountain.
My sister said he probably has
cataracts, and that's perhaps why
he is homeless as well.
I worry that one day he will no
longer be there, many storeys
beneath me —
my blind watchman.

VII.

Last summer me and my wife
went to Rome.
It was so hot, we sheltered in
the Villa Borghese.
My wife has no love for art, so I
wandered the gallery alone.
At the end of a dark room I
saw a sculpture of a woman
crouching with her back to me.
And in that moment, I felt a chill
as though from six feet under
I heard moss growing over
my grave.

VIII.

My father is a miner.
Every day when I was a child he
descended into the earth.
I would often stare at the
pithead ladders
that offered up our town to the sky.
My mother cleaning soot off the
washing line:
particles of earth falling back home.

IX.

I saw in the news about the
floods in Venice.
They were sealing off the crypt
in St Mark's.
Coffins bobbing in lagoon water.
There's nothing that can be done.

X.

I dreamt last night that he was
still alive
and I called out to him across a
thousand leagues, disturbed.
Disturbing the peace in my
disbelief at seeing him again
at the bottom of a pool with a
face made of coral.
When I awoke my bed was wet.
The roof had leaked in the night
dampening my sheets.

XI.

'Landslide tears down mountain
in the Rhondda.'
I read it in the morning paper.
The article was accompanied by a
picture of the flattened hillside:
snapped tree-trunks protruding
from the earth.
Little ankles, like single shoes on
the roadside.

XII.

My mother used to sing to me
when I was small.
Sat on the little stool, foot on the
pedal ready to go.
I didn't know then that piano
meant softly,
but with her voice rising clear and
brittle above that low swell
I was pulled even deeper into its
warm brown notes.

XIII.

Earlier today I spoke to a friend
on the telephone.
He has not been doing well these
past weeks.
Separately we climbed the
scaffold of our conversation.
Words coiling in the air like smoke
from a fire below.
I remember holding the phone
aloft to get signal
just before he cut out.

XIV.

One of my friends in college had
a pack of tarot cards.
People always begged her to
do their readings and one day
she did mine.
We were high and she shuffled
the cards.
The hanged man pinned upside-
down by one ankle.
Like he was doing a jig in mid-air:
a spinning Catherine wheel tied
to a post.

XV.

This weekend my girlfriend and I
are driving to the sea.
We will eat in our favourite
restaurant:
the one with the spinning
fish outside.
Ellie always laughs and says its
being barbecued by the sun.

XVI.
I was reading a poem where
an old king is cursed
by a priest and is turned into
a bird.
The king-poet crosses the island
in one bound, his words following
on the breeze.
Honeyed words, spreading slowly:
like ice or another viscous fluid.

XVII.
Yesterday as I was walking
I came across a lamppost on
which someone had written
'the trees are growing.'
And I had a sudden vision
of branches made of light and
roots of cable:
a whole machine
microbiome.

XVIII.
When I was in my thirties I began
having this recurring dream
of an upside-down lighthouse.
Reflected in the water it looked
the right way up
as though the sky and sea had
changed places.
One day I told my mother about
the dream.
How do you know it is not you
that is the wrong way up,
she asked?

XIX.
As I was leaving the elevator in
my building,
I saw in the lobby a man with
a ladder,
all white from washing windows.
As he dipped his hands in the
bucket to clean them
I tasted slices of soft bread
soaked in sweetened milk.

XX.
Before bed each night my
father would make himself a cup
of hot chocolate.
Measuring out precise spoonfuls
of cocoa into the mug:
he liked it very strong and sweet.
Towards the end of his life I would
have to help him at the stove.
I was not as careful and often
the milk would boil over,
wispy suds flooding the
electric hob.

)

XXI.

Entering the underground on
my way to work
I always felt suffocated.
As the escalator pulled me down,
I felt the heaviness of recycled air,
air so heavy with other people's
saliva that it sinks.
A cloud pushing its tendrils into
mouths and noses, billowing
from orifices.
I felt an updraft as a train went by
at the same time I inhaled
the contents of another's lungs
into my own.

XXII.

I have a photograph of myself
as a teenager,
maybe seventeen years old.
I am mucking about in the lake
near our house,
you can just see my face above
the water.
Starbursts halo my head like I'm
made of light.
After the photo was taken my
brother pulled me under,
water filling my mouth and nose.
I coughed it back up again along
with my own spit and mucus –
globs of foam on the surface.

XXIII.

Today the air-conditioning
broke in the office.
I slipped off to the bathroom
and sat in the stall.
Reaching a hand under my
shirt I wiped away the sweat.
The toilet paper was cheap
and thin and stuck to my hair
in little fibrous pills,
hard and painful to unravel.
Soon the sheet was soft and
wrinkled in my hand,
close to giving up on me.
I flushed it and went back
outside.

XIV.

I read about a man who wore a
photograph strapped under
his shirt.
When he came to take it
off he found
it had transferred onto his
skin like a temporary tattoo.
A boy now smiled up at him
from his ribcage.
Four pairs of eyes, two noses,
two mouths.

Raluca de Soleil

—

expulsare (2011–2021)

they gave her a new name to bury hers
they could smell her from the door
arum flowers grew from her follicles
the sand was burning in her temples
they inhaled and then spat: 'Lori'
Lori: sticking like small condoms
Lori: swaying between their eyes salivating
staring at her ribs
Lori thought she was on stage
playing games of sexual-emotional frustration
in front of imaginary ticket-payers
only breathing for the warmth
of the one she had come for
through invisible magnetic
threads sewn to the thighs
he communicated safety
tacitly telepathically
they laughed at the audience
physical demonstrations
mathematical problems
how much can a back carry at 17
that 30+ dream of bending?
the more his roommates injected
testosterone into the atmosphere
the more Lori tightened her threads
and drew herself closer to the artist
contemplating her from the couch
when finally colliding in private
she felt free yet out of danger
Lori, 17, did not anticipate that 6 months later
she will crumble with her knees on the tiles
she will crack under the weight of 30+
no noise, no fire signals—
guilty of being invaded.

Olly Todd

—

Entonox

It felt like we'd have slipped right off Archway Road
Despite only an apple-roll gradient and millimetric scuff
Of rain, such was our shared vertigo,
Vetoed from triage for not contracting enough,
Walking past A&E with its OD frontier,
Cannula puppets still bidding they smoke,
No attrition for our cupidinous fear
Or the soles of our shoes, not the merest stroke
Of friction. The overfull bus-stop bin;
The unresponsive taxi app; the four-a.m. chill;
The fresh sounds of other women
Straining for established labour's Sangreal;
The lucky, strangled devils who reached theirs well
That night; the U-turning taxi with the road to itself

(

Tilia

Cumbersome in the street lime,
Wood pigeons, back again.
A family out for air, dad in tow,
A weekday. Crunch time. Claws

Of rain on the window. An arsenal
Of tennis balls, Aerobies, Lucozade
Appears wired to them but with the
Consoling manner of biodegradability.

Dad does shorts with a City Boy
Watchcoat. Mum, deprecating, Di-ish
Uplook, straw-weight body a headrace
For the millwheel water

Of their lives, worries her facemask
At the corner by the daily briefing graph
Of a malerected bamboo fence fringing
A terracotta garden wall.   )

Certain shoots – fall
Metrics – telegraphing axis: Pavement
Desiccation Rate. Apparently some guys
Just got to skate, heedlessly

Cramming Daubeney Fields,
Rightly dubbed 'Cummins Bumps'
Now of course. We're out of spirit
Vinegar for the limescale in the loo.

The comb handle won't do.
The lemonyellow comb,
Free in some Qantas Air or
Ozen beach resort welcome pack

Years ago. A work trip would be so
Holy now. What else... needle
And thread, toothbrush and paste,
Single blade razor, eye mask

Stephen Watts

—

And When I Went ...

for Gareth Evans

And when I went
To Close-Up, Gareth was there
And he gave me a white wine &
I blessed him for that, there
Just round from Sclater Street
Where stolen bikes were sold
& Charlie Burns still yawns

And when I went into
'Libreria' on Hanbury Street
Betsy said she was just reading
My 'Republics' and we talked
A mountain about translation
And we shook hands on it
Before I turned to go

And when I went into
'Rough Trade' there was my
Old friend Frank Stanford
In his rare uncollected glee
And I wept at the memory
Of 25 unwasted years

And when I went into
The old Trumans' Republic
To get Turkish spinach börek
I turned away again not because
They are not so good there
But from diffidence at
The Sunday crowds

And when I put my
Head into 'Meraj' on Hanbury
To give my hellos to Shamim,
The proprietor there all these
Years, his cooks took them
And I know that they'll
Have passed them on

And when I turned
Off Brick Lane because
The crowds made it too thick
To walk down & get anywhere
I wandered off on my own
And ended up on Vallance
Opposite the Algerian
Cake shop ...

And when I went to cross
Onto New Road I turned right
Instead & wended up at Indo
As if by trial & magic &
Bought a half measure of
Weiss at the bar

And then who should
Walk in to the empty space
But Tim from Stepney Way
And he insisted on another &
Then he listened to me tell how
Stina'd lost her Ryan as he
Tried to save our world &
He sent her his big hug

)

And when he left
What did the barmaid do
But bring me another half
Over on the house just when
I was least expecting more
Kindness from anyone
But she was glad to

And when I went out
Again onto the sunlit street
Where the air was bright &
Molecules seemed to dance
Their way into a new physics
A new one that might give
Our world another chance

Just then as I went out
The sacred air stopped still
The roadways cleared all traffic
The skies above let out a cry
And joy battered our hearts
In blind Whitechapel of
The hayrick daze

In blind Whitechapel
Where I've lived these forty
Clearly un-hallucinating years
And all the laundered moneys
Went to smoke in high sky-rise
And all conveyances ceased
And peace reigned easily
In blind Whitechapel

And when I went
Round the corner to New
Road & stopped at Needo's
For samosas (1 meat, 1 veg)
My friend of twenty years
Wrapped them with mint &
Refused to take my money

And I didn't know why
Such blessings had come to me
That fine Sunday in August when
The world was in such a bad state
And Stina had just lost her Ryan
But I had been given benisons
Right through the afternoon
In old & blind Whitechapel

My friends I say this to you
Because of the ordinary things,   )
Because the ordinary things of
Our lives do matter & because
Of Avrom Stencl who drank
With the homeless & the holy
Nomads under thorn trees

And as I turned down
Watney beneath the blue
Plane-plume-woven skies
A regal woman passed me &
I returned her upright glance
With my unmercied gaze
So we walked on …

Stephen Watts

And as I turned into
My own yard all the kids
There on their scooters &
Leg-pegs to save the world
With their feet & footballs
Their bicycles & tricycles
Indeed did save the world
As Elsa had predicted

And as I went out again
To Close-Up there again was
Gareth getting me a white wine
& I thanked him & blessed
The day when we could talk
Again in calm wonder at
The foment of the world

(

At the great starry clusters
& Perseid meteor showers
At the ordinary footfalls of
Our premature insanities &
At the forlorn ecstasies of
What we can never attain
Amid the exacted dream-
Births of our compassion.

All of this I dreamed
At home when the world
Seemed about to be ending
And as I went out of dream
Back into my sleep, a rare
Calm settled into my heart
And everything fainted
To a soft pure blue …

Natalie Crick
—
Snow Mam

Lee watches Mam's face for clues
in the living-room mirror.

Her jaw might tense or her smile fix.
Her laughter might spin higher.

She is arranging flowers
in tall glass vases by the bay window.

Frosty spider mams.
Thin thistle mams.

As a little boy Lee had a recurring dream
of Mam: a dark mark on her neck

that swelled until it suffocated her.
Later Mam walks with Lee in the garden.

Snow swirls behind her, her footsteps
like dusts of sugar from too small a crock.

Lee stands still as she walks ahead,
his medicine bag swinging at her hip,

and wonders how a body
could disappear into all that white.

Skipping with Julie

after 'Children and their Stories' by Paula Rego, 1989

Watching Julie skip
Lee reminds himself this is a game
not an adult movie.

As Julie skips, her nipples
jerk under her t-shirt.
At first, Lee's skip is awkward

and he bumps into Julie,
but soon he gets it right.
Children turn in their beds

and join Lee and Julie,
moving in black waves
from the bottom of a ship.

Girls with skipping ropes and hoops.
Boys with baby faces and knock-knees,
torchlit heels showing.

While the children skip
there is a long cold spell.
A harsh frost settles over their play.

When everyone has gone, Lee sits in the hail
thinking of Julie's breasts
and cuts himself
on silver blades of grass.

Dal Kular
—

Race is the least interesting part of me. It
visibilises me and invisibilises me in equal
measure. I prefer being invisible on my own
terms. Like the way the North Sea sculpts
the space between the old man and
mainland, splitting sunsets in two.

I am tired of the same old story. You never
see the other part, the part
that paradiddles bones, soul
dancing by no-light of dark moons.

She's way more dangerous and free, in the
arms of samurai and skulls. Sometimes she
gets lost in the cloud of forgetting,
becomes an invisible veil like that final
breath gifting a palm, waiting. She belongs
to places, wild places. Hurricanes don't
scare her cos she's a big lass now and
survived a few.
Silver strands ride her head,
manicured claws ready to slay and a heart
full of ancient echoes, blood bodies and
resistance, wilderness and not-otherness but
'this-ness'.

This-ness and this creative life.

white pages |

i was creative before i knew i was brown| i created myself female before i was born| that was my first act of creation| & my first act of defiance| my soul is shades of everything| when i was six i wrote about snow-white-men in royal blue ink across off-

(

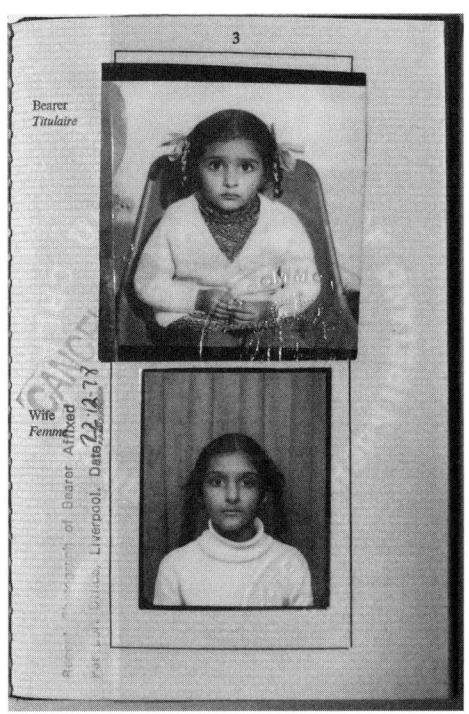

Roisin Dunnett

—

Terrible, Little

Christ is crucified on a cross of lacquered shells on the mantelpiece of this house. Enhancing His agony are the stiff ridges of lacquer and calcium at His back, mortifying Him with the stale smell of the seaside. Someone made this cross for the little figure because he, in his own way, is a maker of offerings.

All around him are the curls and wisps of smoke from his pipe. He makes ships out of shells, spreads glue over pieces of twine to make them taut like rigging. With anal precision he combs beaches for shells of precisely the right size and curvature. Won't buy them by the bag. He admires shelled creatures, which learned before crawling from the sea to hide soft bodies in armour made of coral. We were not so clever, he thinks, and he is right.

Nicotine poisoning, from smoking through prolonged insomnia, 36 hours or more, while beachcomber Christ stared down at him with baleful eyes and asked: 'Why have you cemented me?' He doubled over in the shower, repulsed by the steam which rose off his skin and smelled like the tarry perfume of his pipe as his skin exhaled what his idiot blood had seized and couriered into his vital organs. Heaving again as he came back into his room, smelling the smell of his jacket, his shirts, three pullovers (one navy blue, one forest green, one burgundy), even his socks and his underwear, all freely, gaily, exuding the terrible vapour.

Once returned from hospital he began to set shells around the door, then in the corners of the ceiling. Before long the shells were falling down the walls, and he went around with a bucket of freshly mixed cement and, in a course of months, he stopped the gaps between the drips composed of shells with still more shells until he had covered one whole room, and in time nearly all of his little flat with shells, and the pieces of shells. At that time we had not yet seen the other things which he had made from shells, the fat flightless birds and the coruscated dogs and cats, not to mention the gaping mouth with sharp teeth made of pointed bivalves, the great rose with a thousand petals like little ears, little roundels of cartilage, all cocked and listening.

By the time we came to rescue him, we saw how he had been trying to wall himself in all the way round. Why would you do this, we asked him, how would you get out? And he didn't know. He didn't know his way around his own head that man, the way some people do. He knew a great deal, in some respects, about what had been in the heads of others, and even where in their head the thoughts might have been (he took, at one time, an interest in dream interpretation, and at another time in neuroscience. We thought the preoccupation with the shells would pass, as these pursuits had). But while, after months of absent-minded fasting, in the mirror he could see what we all saw: a skull in sharp relief beneath his skin, it did not occur to him to crack back the hinge on his bone-plate and have a good squint. He differed, in that way, from the rest of us: a family who otherwise were generously (some might say aggressively) therapised. He never asked himself: why do I always do this, or that? Why does this make my heart thump in my chest like a tumbling rock, but not that? Why does this sentimental film make me cry, not that one? How have I chosen (or not chosen) my lovers? He never asked himself those questions.

When we asked him about the impulse to seal up, not just the door but the windows, all possible sources of light, with shells embedded in cement, he had nothing to say. He was afraid, I suppose, to find out what had come unstuck, a man who took such pride in clean, modest suits and good but simple cooking for a bachelor and his occasional guests. I once sat at his table and watched him drink enough to make a person unconscious (more than enough to make me vomit in his bathroom sink) but, when he stood up to show me out, even his eyes were steady.

When it came to moving his things from the flat when he died, what I found worst were the terrible little animals which by that time covered all the shelves and were lined up along all of the skirting boards. Tiny teeth, made of shells, the fur whorled stiff with little points and the perfect spirals of shells, bright glass eyes in orange and yellow staring madly out of the mercilessly sharp definition of frames formed by the edges of shells.

He never became hard-shelled himself. More like, if anything, some variety of deep-sea slug. I think of the soft foot, tenderly feeling the contours of everything. Their great luminous finery: frills and barbs and polka dots, their many colours. Hiding from view in the great big hush of the ocean.

He once gave me, for a young birthday, a green beetle in a box. It was very dead, but he had unpinned it from its piece of labelled card and put it in with leaves and twigs and a little dish. The box had a transparent lid with air holes. My mother was polite, but confused, maybe irritated. A dead beetle (green and shining) in a box? But my father, the youngest sibling, outgoing and the most resilient, put his arm around the shoulders of my uncle, and they both looked down at me, who did not notice, because I was staring down at this beetle, electric green and shining.   )

My father: 'Say thank you.'

Me: (shifting the box a little, side to side) 'Thanks.'

James Conor Patterson
—
LET ME TAKE YOU DOWN 'CAUSE I'M GOING

You're sitting in an office at the back of a jeweller's shop on Lord St. The office shares a floor with the Thai consulate and every so often a woman sticks her head around the door to check if you're alive. She's wearing an indigo & blood-red uniform in the manner of an air hostess and she's not smiling. On the desk in front of you is a bracelet made from paper clips. On your computer monitor is a still from the documentary *The Million Pound Necklace*.

Three times a day you fantasise about robbing the place. You internalise the shop's layout in your mind, visualising how it would be to skulk around the silent hallways after dark with the orange glow from the streetlights pooling in through the window. You'd wear a black balaclava, jumper, black trackies and trainers.

You think about the cat burglar Molloy, from *The Simpsons*, and wonder how he got around complex problems like alarm systems and security cameras. Ultimately, you decide that the whole thing is implausible, despite the fact that you know the door codes. As the jeweller's newest employee, suspicion would invariably fall upon you, and anyway—who do you know in the black market for diamonds?

The reason you fantasise like this isn't because you're new, or on a temp contract, or underpaid. It's because you're an admin; someone whose job it is to read about & photocopy glamorous CV after glamorous CV, making shortlists of candidates with qualifications in subjects like Gemmology, then handing them over to your manager based on how far below £40k they're willing to drop.

You do this for 20 hours a week, supplementing fallow periods when you have no money with freelance blogging jobs, newspaper articles, explainer video scripts and the occasional short story. You write these at £100 a pop for *Ireland's Own*, under the *nom de plume* Seamus Ó Ruaidh. Stories about Shane McGowan-esque emigrants boarding the ferry at Roslare. Stories about homeless men on the streets of Liverpool with hearts of gold. Stories you wouldn't normally allow yourself to become sentimentalised by, but which in recent times have taken on new meaning.

Everything now is seen through the lens of what you've left behind and Liverpool's Irish pubs no longer seem kitsch. The GAA matches they show no longer seem boring and, in fact, are manifestations of an idealised life in miniature. Soft reminders of what you could be doing at home, where jobs are plentiful, the pints are thick & free-flowing and the sun (conversely) never refuses to shine.

* * *

Pogue's is ground zero for the Irish in Liverpool. The place where you're as likely to fall into conversation with a construction worker from Tyrone as you are with a hen do on a weekend away from Clonmel. And because it's become a kind of respite for you during your two years away from home, you're faintly charmed by its down-at-heel glamour. Blowing thick layers of concrete dust & ash off the bar stools. Standing among throngs of sweaty GAA jerseys on match day. Drinking questionable whiskey branded after & promoted by the bar. You think of it as *Cheers* without a permanent license. An ever-shifting centre of gravity with changes in ownership, occasional closures, piss-stained bathroom tiles and its own football team.

One of your first times there, you fall into conversation with the barman after filling out a registration form for the postal vote.

Who are you voting for?

I'm not sure yet. What do you think yourself?

Up the Shinners, he says.

This was back in 2017 when Jeremy Corbyn surprised everyone by denying Theresa May the parliamentary majority she expected to win so comfortably. And though much has changed since then, much hasn't. You're still no clearer now on the status of the Irish border than you were before the Brexit vote, and many Irish people in Britain are in the precarious position of not knowing what their rights will be. As for those returning to Ireland at Christmas or Easter, it's unclear how easy it'll be to travel. So they're in limbo. A feeling you know only too well.

* * *

Your relationship with Britain is complicated. Despite the fact that Irish Republicanism runs in your blood like a genetic predisposition to freckles, several times during your life you've found yourself on the wrong side of the Irish Sea. Two years in Liverpool. Six years as a child in Aberdeen. A recent move to London.

At various points during the 1950s and '60s, all four of your grandparents spent time living and working in England. Your ma spent the first fourteen years of her life in Birmingham, and after she married your da, they lived in a single bedroom flat in the shadow of Highfield Road in Coventry—the city where you were born.

Nevertheless, your move to Liverpool feels like a big deal. A number of factors play into the conversations you have with your girlfriend about finding a place to settle, but chief amongst them is the notion that Liverpool is somehow more Irish than the rest of England.

Your grandda once told you about how Churchill and De Valera met during the Second World War, and how whilst negotiating a potential break in Ireland's neutrality, De Valera asked Churchill when he would give back the six counties.

We'll give back the six, Churchill said, when you give back Liverpool.

So that's where you end up—Ireland's 33rd county in exile—where for two years you convince yourself that you haven't really *gone* anywhere. The flight to Dublin only takes half an hour, after all, and the majority of conversations you have with Scouse taxi drivers tend to culminate with the phrase, me gran's from Wexford, or me dad came over on the boat from Belfast.

And yet, for everything that makes you feel close to home, you can't shake the feeling that you've somehow been displaced. Council tax isn't a financial consideration you had to make in Newry or Belfast, and the tea bags in England somehow make a brew which tastes like pencil shavings. Little things remind you that despite your proximity to a *sort of* Irishness, you're still an outsider. Your accent still marks you out as a source of mild derision, and several times during your stay in the city even provokes outright prejudice.

* * *

The first time it happens you're working as a receptionist at a Catholic girls' school in Toxteth. Your job consists of ferrying dilapidated boxes filled with student records up to the front office and transferring them manually onto the school's HR system. You don't mind. The time alone allows you to conceptualise short stories in your pocket book, and free access to the desktop which allows you to conduct any research you need to undertake.

The Head—an elderly nun from Portadown—seems approachable enough and a number of the teachers speak with Irish accents. This is good and confirms to you—for the short term at least—that working in a low-maintenance job might be a way of not only giving you space for your writing but making friends as well.

A month or so into the job, you're finishing the last of a bunch of records labelled *Da—Do* and are about to step out for lunch. Another one of the receptionists comes into the office and begins a long, rambling story about an argument she's just had with one of the teachers. Something innocuous about an absence, or a SEN councillor, or the clerical silverware needing to be washed before tomorrow's assembly. All is relatively lighthearted until it becomes clear that she's talking about one of the Irish teachers.

I'll bomb yer fuckin house, she says in a cod-Gerry Adams accent. Wouldn't be surprised if she did, the little tart. Certainly has anger issues. Got to be an IRA connection somewhere.

The other receptionists—who are all women in their fifties—start laughing. Someone says something about watching her back. Another is so choked with mirth that her forehead glistens and her cheeks bulge with trapped air. The woman telling the story is now rabbiting on about something else, but by this point your ears are so hot and filled with blood that you can't hear what she's saying. Suddenly, one of the receptionists notices you're in the room and the laughter stops. She turns to you.

I wouldn't take tha, she says, pointing to the storyteller.

I'd take er outside if it were me.

Show er who's boss.

Everyone laughs again. The tension momentarily breaks.

I would take her outside, you say, turning to the room. But she's Scouse, she'll probably do me with a fuckin' knife.

Nobody laughs this time. It soon becomes clear that unless you're on the fag-end of a joke about coming from somewhere rough, stereotypes aren't acceptable. It's better for you to know your place and stay in it.

Where that place *is* exactly is a question which hangs over you the entire time you're in Liverpool.

* * *

During your stay you experience two more incidents like this. Once, when an old man overhears your accent and tells you & your girlfriend to *fuck off home, scum*. And once when you're in an Uber after a night out and the driver points to a snooker ball-sized scar on the back of his hand.

 I know Newry, he says. Took a bullet there in '96 while I was out on patrol. Locals stood and fuckin' watched me.

 This isn't the norm, of course, and for the most part your interactions with Scousers make you proud to share their city. Like the time an illustrator gives you his old bike so you can get to your job more easily. Or the barber on Aigburth Road who—having once been a soldier himself—talks about how disillusioned he became with the establishment and how his love of Ireland grew after he left the Army. The radio presenter who sends you a list of job recommendations when you move to London, and the taxi driver who drops you off outside Krazyhouse and waives your fare.

 Me dad was Jamaican and me mum was Irish, she says. And both communities need to look out for each other. Especially in this country. Remember tha.

 In fact, what keeps you in the city for so long is the abundance of kindness you experience when you're there. Like in 2016, when you witnessed residents protest for the removal of anti-homeless architecture on Castle St. Or the camaraderie you experienced in the lead-up to the 2017 Champions League final—which Liverpool lost to Real Madrid—and the unshakeable faith that next year would be *the* year, *our* year, after so many years of disappointment.

 You love the independence & defiance of the place. The fact that it declared itself a Nuclear Free Republic in the 1980s then staged the biggest strike in a decade after 500 Dockers were dismissed by Liverpool Port Authority in 1995. You love its passion for sport and its love of music. Its dozens of record shops, vintage clothes stores, independent mags, radical bookshops and cheap pizza parlours. The smell of Lebanese food wafting into Bold St on a hot summer's day. The brainfreeze of a cheap bottle in the back room of Keith's on Lark Lane. Sefton Park. The coffee in 92 Degrees. Your gorgeous, fucking freezing Georgian flat with black mould and a marble fireplace in the living room. Your Jack Russell Chihuahua. Your awkward, brilliant, nerdy-ass pal from Salford. Your girlfriend who gave you the gift of Liverpool in the first place.

* * *

When you finally leave, perhaps the oddest thing you end up missing is the Magical Mystery Tour. In two years you take it four times, and despite the fact that you've always *liked* The Beatles, the tour for you has little or nothing to do with their music. Taking it is about the ease with which you can fill an afternoon with visiting family or friends, giving them a feel for the place you've come to know & love.

The first time you take it, you've been out the night before with your cousin. The brown sauce smell of stale Jaeger is general on your clothes, and when the bus leaves the Albert Dock your cousin falls asleep in the seat beside you. You're hungover, the weather is miserable, and as you pull out from Keel Wharf onto Chaloner St, Liverpool Cathedral looms blackly over the city.

You come through Dingle, then Toxteth, then onto Princes Drive. The tour guide is saying something about The Beatles having recorded their first song as session musicians for Tony Sheridan, but you aren't really listening. All you can think about is the fact that this city—the city you chose—produced some of the greatest musicians in history. Musicians surrounded by the humdrum ordinariness of postwar Britain. Musicians who celebrated that ordinariness through songs like 'Strawberry Fields Forever', 'Penny Lane', 'Eleanor Rigby' and 'In My Life'.

As you pass by Sefton Park, you see the bandstand which supposedly inspired the concept for *Sgt. Pepper*. You realise that Liverpool's ordinariness is the very thing that makes it remarkable. Not ordinary in the sense of featureless or dull, but the kind of ordinary envisioned by utopians—where community has the capacity to nurture, talent is seen in the context of the environment which allowed it to thrive, and *home* is predicated on the idea that no matter how far you go, you always have somewhere to come back to.

When the tour finally finishes two and a half hours later, you clamber off the bus onto Lord St, where you'll later take a job as an admin in a jeweller's shop. You stumble towards The Cavern, which—like visiting ley lines—has re-energised you, and after spending the day trying to stave off the fear, you're finally ready for another pint.

Your cousin asks if Liverpool is somewhere you could see yourself settling long-term.

And you say no. You're not sure you'd ever fully be able to settle in England.

But in the years & months since, you come to realise that Liverpool never really felt like England at all. That sense of community you so badly wanted to access, that sense of displacement at being both from elsewhere & no longer able to go home, that proximity to an artistic heritage forged in the everyday—you've never felt those things before or since. Not in Coventry, not in Aberdeen, not Newry, Dublin, Belfast or London. Liverpool offered a way of finding oneself amid a myriad of contradictions. A way of mourning the past *and* improving upon it, all the while cultivating a deep uncertainty about the future. Such things are bad for one's sense of placement but good for art. Such things can sometimes produce miracles.

Karen Whiteson

—

Runaway Film

She's sitting by a table near the window from where she keeps one eye on the lecture hall door and the other on the TV monitor to its right. Via its screen she can make out preparations for the symposium within; the desultory bustle of the techies milling about the huddle of speakers, as they confer upon the podium.

He is there, amongst the latter group, signalling collegiate affability from the distant stage.

Framed as she is by a wall-to-ceiling window behind her, she has half-consciously positioned herself in such a way so that, should he emerge, he'd see her sitting in moody profile against the glass rectangle; now rapidly growing dark as late autumn evening creeps in.

The knowledge that he remains oblivious of her gaze makes for an uneasy pleasure. She knows that any advantage this gives will be overturned the moment he comes through the door, into the antechamber. Anticipating the moment, she has surrendered herself to the posture of the woman who waits; without the props of phone or book, or the alibi of any companion. Her hope is that he might recognise – in the disposition of her limbs, in the angle of her neck, in the patience engraved in the corners of her eyes – the obduracy of some absurd truth. Though there is, she realises, no certainty he will emerge. At that very instant (as if her vigil was about to be rewarded) the screen shows him leaving the podium and making towards the exit. She waits for him to step out of the frame before she lets herself look left and he bursts through the door looking straight at her, as if he'd known all along she was sitting there. Neither flinches, though both partake of an equal astonishment. Felled by his crystalline glance she sees his veering off in a sharp right, in the direction of the toilets.

She recalls how the first-ever cinema-goers, on viewing the Lumière Brothers' footage of a locomotive entering the station, bethought themselves so caught up in the path of its approach that they all rushed for the exit. And, how this founding myth of cinema – where the real breaks through the virtual with a diagonal force of verisimilitude sufficient to unleash a stampede in the theatre – has no foundation. Not only was the picture in black-and-white and with a salient flicker, but it had no soundtrack, and so was unlikely to have provoked such credulity. There exists not one contemporary account that might corroborate this legend of a film which runs away with itself, dislodging itself from the screen, to pervade the auditorium.

(

GRAVITY BUBBLES

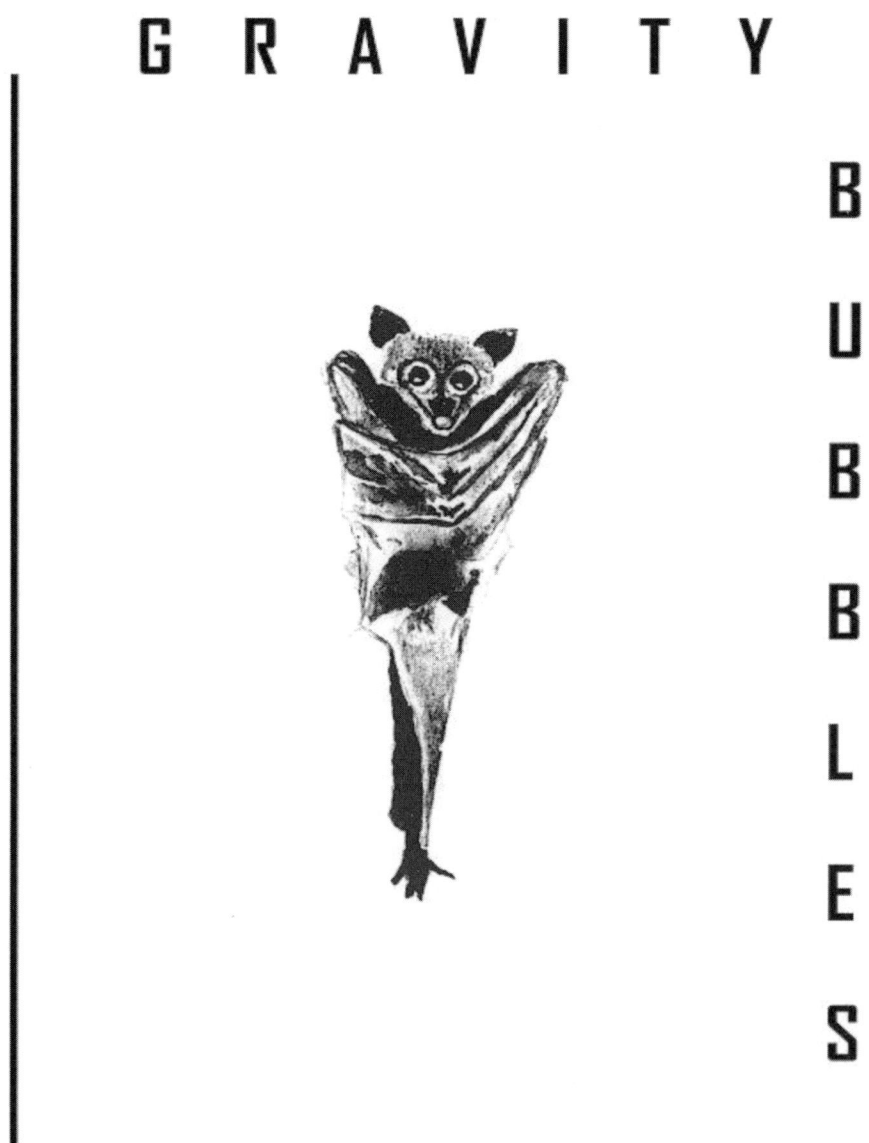

Marcus Slease
Calliope Michail
Chris Gutkind
Spring 2020

                people sitting in cars going nowhere

cracked windows in ubers; one frozen ear at work

                ```
people walking in circles, on the rooftops,
              around and around the chimneys
```

                I heard apparently was true again

to be both at once and act just so

                ```
buckwheat bread & veggies fried in breadcrumbs
```

                outside and inside meet/eyes more than screens

pigeons and preachers rule the streets

                ```
the sound of rhinos snorting and stomping,
         above and below, all around them
```

                pajamas obey each other/evolve a shop crawl

who do you wear a bra for

                ```
Become superfluous like swatches of silk
```

                our ears amok our nears unakimbo

inarticulate tendrils an infernal limbo

                ```
a small train drifting through the mountains,
                   a smok in the distance
```

                fettered fucked blending detime.decom

strangers on omegle modern romcom

                    I'd like a yellow onion, on the mountain,
                                            with the sea air

           love! love! all my comms for love..

        meanwhile *he's alive!* vs thousands of dead

           I've never walked so slowly gladly..

        meanwhile bark and hark strudel pompomly

and then and now and then

time warps lost parallels collide

orotund headlines pierce through otoliths

monoliths and obelisks, how soft
and can they crumble?

                              Oktoberfest is cancelled
                    the strudels have disappeared
                              from Spanish bakeries
                    all my dreams are adolescent
                                            & wet

      shadows of light unseen keep going me warpy

the always banal, the sheets, the dishes, the body

        if you blast the light inside you you beam

        the milk problem – but the milk joy !
          and the Hammershoi crease !

you shower and read and the psocids
stroke their mandibles

                    a woman in black her back turned
                       a woman in black pouring milk

        I used to be mandibled a lot
        until mass unemployment

bled white rice and pinto beans – what more
could you want, goes grandma's yoke

                    my ghosts have gone underground

        I see you speak ventilator well
        but how is your mask

on the tip of my tongue, a tickle trapped

            the sound of the bell that leaves the bell

        once upon a tipple all the bank's accounts
        and all the bank's kin couldn't put
        tongues together again

i$ there any lint in Bezo$' pocket$?
what $hape i$ hi$ $oul?

                            We are in a pickle

        could he doth be formed of virus
        ancients saw gleeing by the shitpile?

windowsill scene: skull decanter rotting wine a plastic white rose

            here comes the llama, the llama has the cure,
                        the llama has the antibodies

        Every angel is terrifying.
        You must change you life.

combat the invisible – biology and flaming swords

                        `Belgium is moving to social bubbles`

        an upsidedown bucket a hood to unsee thru
        there's a hole in bucket UK dear Boron dear Boron

clap and unwind in the countryside
a baby a lady 5 cobras

                                          `when are we gonna`
                                                        `break out`
                                                   `of our stables`

                wake news eat news
             others news comms news
              wash and dress news
              tea again comms news
               stretch maybe news
               maybe writing news
              maybe read book news
              new news water news
                more eating news
              maybe walking news
                more comms news
               helping a bit news
              snoozing maybe news
               wishing time news
                tea news tea news
             memory memory news
                worry dream news
              out wandering news
                shop maybe news
               writing maybe news
              phonecall maybe news

         more eating news
         vidcall maybe news
         alcohol like news
         nice old old film ah
         news teeth bed

whale fuse beat fuse
otters fuse combs fuse
bash and bless fuse
sea again combs fuse
belch maybe fuse
maybe biting fuse
maybe feed cook fuse
fuse fuse matter fuse
sore bleating fuse
maybe stroking fuse
maybe maybe fuse combust

                              a stye in the eye
                           duck tape the tear ducts

         I need to stroke otters right away

              Meanwhile in England..

dolly croons on google earth
elon is devoting himself to mars
where the newborn will morph
into an elven spacecraft
and there's no more room for s/words
in my stomach or my head

just you wait and see

      bionic beavers, count the sheevers

the crack of doom is coming soon

    you want herdle no problem
    lots of herdles about these days
    gov't fuckwits a herdle to life
  herdles of delivery vehicles to avoidle
      tons of herdles starting again
    can get you a herdle in an hour
      herds of fingers in morgues

virtual cycling let's go!

    buttermilk biscuits in white gravy
      saucy lime with a gin fizzle
      they've shaved their stashes

minuscule cracks in the window glass
cobwebs scramble neural index

    to your own smile.com be uncom
    especially if you have rulers

  besotted with clotted cream and the dainty finger

eudemons, dysdemons, somewhere in the shuffle

           after I was in a doze of aisledom
           I wash my grocers and read a movel

```
                   when you eat the smile of a watermelon
                         make sure to spit out the seeds
```

watch the bees enter and exit and enter
petalled coves of nourishment - here,
still searching - what season is this

                on the wall two words
                   near the ground
                      written small
                        cry alone

```
                        isolation is losing its lustre
                   we need more flesh for our existence
```

vonate matterial suprotest & topple it all

        every/one   every/place   infinite

```
        life: on/off on/off on/off on/off on/off
   life: with infinite time all life in the repeat
   life: with finite time all life in the twilight
```

& beyond - love in a plate of nightshades

     twilife: *we missed the McD's sweet and sour sauce!*

```
        Do you want to die with your original teeth
```

the loudest voice isn't always just

     coffee frothies are strutting less gleamy..

```
        The shadows of birds flit across the window
```

pirouettes on melting ice cubes

    le people are ££'ing to the slaughter

        `lavender oils in the mop bucket`

just because _____ doesn't mean _____ .

    I forgot I started my conversations with myself

        `On the back of a motorcycle carrying`
            `feathers across the borders`

ok ok, see, not a paradigm,
see shift ctrl alt del

    i came across a statue who told me
    he genuinely understood he erased history
    and then contributed to the death of 44
    London Transport workers during
    the last months – but he said he was glad
    he could remain useful and alive

    trying to become one with the music of Haydn,
something about a bear, maybe there is something
    in there, the cabbage stewing in onions and
mushrooms with sausages for bigos, a little jungle
    of plants in the room beside the balcony

every monument some
horror somewhere too much
bronze and marble and not enough—

    too much sausages of jungles
    and plants of tryings while onions
    of music make calls and leases of become

```
The Venus of Willendorf is a sex statue to fertility.
        The Pigeon Girl is a statue to war sufferings.
The Urfa Man is the oldest statue of a life sized homo
            sapien. When did all the generals arrive?
```

it boils, the becoming, up
and then down into pulp
a jam or a sauce, a patchy
teflon pan, all the scraping injested

reproduction boil statue:

```
                    tweeting the quench quakes
```

wei_h & e_punge the ha_vest of abys_al po_osity

all along the restarting twitts are roamy –
many a jerk brew a poisonous batch!

110

                        The watchtower the watchtower
                        who is watching the watchtower

centrefold days unfurl your limbs

                    I'm feeling interfood today,
                    tomorrow I'm to feel like like.

                    - Christopher are you okay?

                    - Yes, reporting for duty!

            Inhale for five second exhale for five seconds
                                    comrades friends lovers
                        this is how we walk on the moon

hefty babes in dainty cradles -
report me. report me. report

                Inhale: Saudi oil quarterly profits down a quarter
                        to only 16.64 billion USD!

                        Exhale: boo-hoo..

    The way is lit by the luminous eyes of my billy goat

ordering options

option 1
Full sequence of CM/CG, then full of MS/CG, the former first since it started first.
Alternate 1a – run each one backwards

option 2
First part of CM/CG sequence till switchover, then first part of MS/CG till switchover, then second part of CM/CG sequence till end, then second part of MS/CG till end.
Alternate 2a – do this backwards in one of various ways

option 3
CG/CM first exchange, CG/MS first exchange, CG/CM second exchange, CG/MS second exchange, etc
There may be more than one CM/CG or MS/CG in a row since that is so at end of first and second parts.
Alternate 3a – run this backwards

option 4
CG's first thing, CM's first thing, MS's first thing, etc
There may be more than one CM/CG or MS/CG in a row since that is so near end of first and second parts. CG would have to decide on the few different versions of his contribs to each of you.
Alternate 4a – run this backwards

option 5
This incorporates a 4th person. This person acts as editor, they take all our work (I would make mine half its size, so just one of each of my repeated things and I decide on which revision of any where there are diffs), and puts it in any order they want, not changing any word or word order within a person's contribution, simply making the order they think is strongest and taking all our names out, we would know which is our bit, the reader would not.
option 5a – we colour-code it and provide a key, so reader knows who did what.
option 5b - which could be used with either of the above – a constriction whereby the editor must always place a different person's contribution after another i.e. no repeated person.

option 6
This also incorporates a 4th person. Basically we take option 4 and ask a person to do their own 32 contribs and slot them in wherever but never more than one person's at a time. Or some such thing.
Operates without our names like option 5, revealed or not in end-notes.
option 6a – 4th person makes their contribs but we slot them in
option 6b – run this backwards after they/we are done

option 7
Put parts in a hat..
option 7a – run this backwards

option 8
Get 4th person to do option 6 but using the text on this page.

option 9
Marcus suggests whatever we do we have this at the end.

option 10

Notes

love! love! all my comms for love, Shakespeare detourn

Every angel is terrifying, from Rilke Duino Elegy 1
You must change your life, from Rilke Archaic Torso of Apollo

there's a hole in the bucket, old song, author unknown

BACK TO WORK / CATCH THE VIRUS / SAVE THE BILLIONAIRES,
one of many satires of UK gov't advice posters, citation lost

just you wait and see, from (There'll be Bluebirds Over) The White Cliffs of Dover,
lyrics by Nat Burton, heard the Vera Lynn recording coming from
a high window on 75th VE Day anniversary 8/5/20

the crack of doom... from a song by the Tiger Lillies

herdle stanza, echo of Big Lebowski film, John Goodman dialogue, in last lines

to your own smile.com be uncom, Shakespeare detourn

we missed the sweet and sour sauce!, from Guardian article, 20/5/20

coffee frothies, from Will Self, 'coffee frothy economy' in a Kakfa talk online, 19/5/20

44 London Transport workers, from TFL website in Spring, will have grown

JUST THE TWEETS book, for sale outside Trump's Tulsa speech, 20/6/20, citation lost

all along the restarting twitts are roamy, a line from Dylan's
All Along The Watchtower was in mind

many a jerk brew a poisonous batch!, a line from Lynch's film,
What Did Jack Do? was in mind

Inhale line stats, from Guardian article, 12/5/20

Title-page design and illustration by Calliope Michail

Ziddy Ibn Sharam

—

from *The Rubaiyat of Ziddy Ibn Sharam*

When you hit me
      hit me hard
ruby riot / rubai'i of finesse   dub
      atomic time unisons

Horror   pilation
      dancing in the snow
unsure what would happen if
      we just left the city

Uprooted in stasis
      & falling apart
in the bedroom
      starved of thrill

(

We meet each other
      under an earthing blanket
with cold January eyes
      the wonderful year.

Let me sink into my heels
      beside Himalayan pine
Croydon has been eating glass
      and this suburb is dying

— I heard limericks at the public house
      Everyone wants to be a poet
all of your favourite philosophers
      the bus driver & the postal clerk

Support groups are full of relapse
  all of us seeking closure
& it finally has come to this
  tobacco and instant coffee on delivery

Every month is cruel
  an amorphic totality
or dissension as extensity
  macaronic yet unreticulated–

Forced to listen to mondegreens
  of robert frost and philip larkin
the nadirs of new movement orthodoxy
  we need a revival to forfend

I miss when we used to sing
  about poetry
and not the digital self projects
  who are called '*the* poets'   )

Please outline your research methodology
  hold the hand of the general reader
stroke the back of the nonspecialist academic
  dumb and dumb*er* entombed in crystal

I dug a thousand more graves
  to escape the old routines
a mantra of honour in the break
  to evade being vehicular for capital

The horizons were green
  at midnight blue with life
all I saw was dust from construction sites
  those works of perdition

Ziddy Ibn Sharam

Preternatural blandishments encased
        by the alacrity of neonicotinoids
wittering those supervenient couvades
        of prime scissile rhythmic couplets

Flesh is the history I'm interned in
        and against its concrescence
we binge-watch the serial
        in enmity towards postmodernity

Obscurantist ethnonationalists by the canals
        self-sensical as a cynosure
whimsy of the broad church
        ego run riot in the liberal psyche

Without accession to the new towers
        watching on in silent disarray
poems taken from twitter threads
        are not the same as ictus prima facie

(

Of nostalgia with the flag-waving idiōtēs
        in such extremity we face dilemmas
what to be done but a re-technē
        not-yet moored against the doubt of choice

Past aural kinetic melody in the spirit
        to be authoritative against semblance
of authority which erased our trace from record
        the centre will never hold us

To be home again
        strong in the grasp
I haven't felt like this
        restored and pissed off

I worry that I spend
        too much time
thinking of what
        others think about me

Order the pizza
        flatten the curve
blog about blogging
        read the images

I have a call now
        sorry if my connection
is unstable or paranoid
        how is it now?

)

Otis Mensah

–

The Look

Just a silent squark
under a raised brow scowl
and we were nothing more than illicit idlers in our playrooms
we knew we would be here forever
tearing and tearing perfect little squares into the silk skies
made for our tiny heads of passion
kept at mountain distance
hawk-eying their decry
and us, a repugnant tease deflowered by naive hue
in all our deformities and unmalleabilities

relinquishing everything
renouncing the sphered world under our feet
commencing the big melt
(until but rusted shavings and oil-spilled puddles of us are left
scaling their chimneys and nostril walls
being at the tip of their every wheeze
surfing the huff and puff fired at our clandestine rituals of self-expression
as if obscene flagellation
but we were just speaking in pretty
rhyming for bread
trying to see more of ourselves in the window of another

Sam Fuller

—

from *Raw Ideas*

'Masculinity fails all bodies even those who wield it, nobody wins when hegemonic masculinity starts to become a straitjacket for a national culture'
– Ocean Vuong

Part I

2.

it being my first time i am more than a little embarrassed to share with you the factual details of our encounter, so i will offer you my interpretation of that memory which would survive one thousand concussions. // She stared at me, her gaze intensely fixed. It was a look which commandeered control of the situation and insisted her decision was the correct one and i was little more than an accessory to a task which had required much consideration. // My entering of her happened shortly after and was quite the opposite of what i had expected from the various accounts i'd read. Rather than taking anything sacred away from her which, it had occurred to me, was the intention of those whom i now regard as unscrupulous types, it empowered and uplifted her, in a way i could scarcely have dreamt possible. // In arriving at our destination, which neither of us had before reached yet both knew intimately, we scribed, at the same moment, an etching onto each other's being which could not be erased

8.

i know i shouldn't but i do. i know what you'd say and i agree but i still would. It is hard to say why but if you knew   it would change how you see me. How i see me changes every day — i don't mean in the mirror. i'm becoming a different person. i can't — have you ever looked at an old photo of yourself and felt a disconnect? Imagine the disconnect is so large it might as well be a different person. My memories feature the old me as a separate being and somehow i can remember things in the third person. i can remember being somewhere and watching that version of me doing something and i've got memories of my own reactions to the things that i did. it hurts my head. i'm scared for the future in case this separation happens again and there exists three of me — then what? Who is to say it won't keep happening until i lose my mind and there are so many versions of myself i can't keep count and i forget which one is the real me? i keep taking photographs but it's futile. i need to reconcile who i am versus who i was and who i am becoming and align the three into one straight line. Maybe then i can sew them together so even when they shift it'll only be like the corners of a triangle moving about the page changing angles but always remaining inherently a triangle with no danger of adopting a different shape

(

Part II

4.

i rewatch memories through a modern lens and judge my actions, anticipating my own future scandal. An intimate touch is appropriate depending on the intent and the recipient's experience. Everything is blurred. Have i forgotten what i didn't want to remember? A beach fumble intertwines with a hand cupping my eleven-year-old penis whilst watching a black-and-white film. How do i separate being touched from touching? Both were okay, weren't they? Consensual at least. Wouldn't either of them [me] have said otherwise? Would i have changed my mind if i could?

1.

& in time i wonder why i think the way i do, why i feel the need to dominate, to be the aggressor, when that's not really me, is it? Or is it a part of me like my heart that i have no control over? Can't i change it? But there's a part of my brain that has this insatiable desire to   — maybe i'm the problem, but what's the solution? How do i fix something i have no control over? By refusing my nature, by refusing to allow the voices in my head to affect me when i feel „emasculated"? But they're already in my head. How do you evict   from your brain? Maybe i'll buy a pink tutu and become a gay cliché 'til it's okay to say hey let's stay in tonight it's quite alright don't swallow or spit i'll do that thing to your clit with my tongue and we'll both have fun without either of us feeling degraded or lesser than one half of a whole

)

Part III

20.

& what then? When she sees what he has constantly covered up like a bed sheet too small for a mattress, what will she say? Will she leave him, as he deserves? Or will she remain loyal, steadfast in the face of everything she isn't, knowing that her life will always contain a stain that bleach and scourers could never remove even at the expense of layers of skin. What then

40.

it wasn't that he was hypercritical or impossible to please, but rather that, at every available opportunity, he encouraged her to do whatever it was that she was doing but at a lesser percentage; to modify her actions in a way that would mean bending her own will around others in quite the same way that a mother's hips bend to accommodate an infant: to comfort and appease. It was the cumulative effect, the constant repetition of requests which turned the insignificant into an almighty issue that he did not for the life of him see coming

42.

there's an authentic fraudulence in his ability to insert recently-learned French phrases into premeditated social situations in which he finds himself talking to attractive women who happen to be endeared by what others would call his 'chat'. Highlights include his lamenting the lack of *jouissance* in certain contemporary situations, which of course leads to a general decline in *joie de vivre*, especially for *le deuxième sexe*, segueing nicely into the story about his difficult childhood

J L Hall

Nocturne

I love the shush of cars in the rain
    and how the words whisper when I turn a page
        beneath the hum and blink of an unseen plane.
            The knife of the gulls' cry in the never dark night;
        a violent peach and

as beautiful as a bruise.

La Laguna Azul

My mother lies in the blue lagoon
In a one-piece swimsuit of lapis lazuli
To hide the hysterectomy wounds
With pleats around the bust
Perspiring beneath
Fresh sunscreen and lipstick
A slick of Avon's Coral Shimmer
Painted on an *I am relaxing* smile
A *don't disturb* smile.

But it isn't a lagoon
Only concrete painted ecru
Sloping slowly into liquid blue
Lapping to an islet of bougainvillea
And palms in a Costa resort.
I wiggle my toes in the shallows
Far away, squinting in the high noon sun
At the one-piece swimsuit with
A twist at its heart.

Oliver Sedano-Jones

—

Birth

'Is' and 'is like' can be very different

Being born *is* one person sprouting from another

But it *is like* an orange tree crying real orange tears
When I was born I cried also

I should have said Good Evening
Or: Mind If I Drop In?
But I thought I'd start as I meant to go on

It was like cliff-diving into a dish of sea anemones
It was like watching the anemones open and close, close and open
Until a single sodden bee crawled out

(

Some things get born and it'd be better if they didn't

Not people. I mean the things between them
I knew one that seemed to love it: born and reborn perpetually
One slimy, shrieking mess after the other

Enough please, I said more than once
But life finds a way, to quote Jeff Goldblum

It was like rescuing a fish from the ocean
It was like removing a cucumber from a hot fridge

Once,
Someone gave birth to some love and pushed it towards me
But I can't give birth myself so I didn't return it
I wanted to and then I didn't
This should be easy to understand but it isn't

Some things are born only from necessity
Like weaving a wig from your own thinning hair

Someone must have needed to bear that love
If it was pushed towards me
Maybe it was meant for someone other than me
Someone who was just a little bit like me at that time
And 'is' and 'is like' can be so very different

So:
Being born is *like* cracking an egg into a waffle toaster
But it's just a doll with another doll inside it

Once,
Someone gave birth to someone else and put me inside them
But the person I was inside couldn't seem to learn even the basics of loving
Like a balloon with a face painted on
I thought I was one thing but turned out to be another

)

It was like throwing a bucket of blood at a Caravaggio
It was like growing flesh artichokes in a vat of expectation

I know I should offer this person some reply
But I'm busy writing this poem now
This poem's going to be born instead

It's being sent down to Earth right now to be born
Like Sharon Olds in 'After Making Love in Winter'
The baby will be rags of red chiffon
The mother will be the sky's pale hem

I should reply, I should return the gift
Only now my pot plants are flowering

Sun is folding into the leaves of the tulip buds
And the purple hyacinth's silly loops
Are broken trumpets flaring against spring

The Ryan Poem

The sky's good intentions fractured
Into liquid pearls as I thought of the famous Ryan
Whose hips I wanted to wear like a leg napkin
I thought of Ryan, imagined him wrapped around me
Like a celebrity vacuum cleaner
Hoovering the arousal right out my mouth
But then I started to picture a different Ryan
Neither Gosling nor Reynolds but a glorious in-between
For whom I'd felt something like love
Lying on the cold diamond shingle of Depression Island
My therapist at that time was also called Ryan
He wanted me to live on a yoga mat forever
Palms like two warm sirloins cooking on my eyes
Watching my thoughts tumble like chimpanzees
In a blazing jungle made of fingers
My inner Ryan would shout at me to do something
But I didn't know what that something was
I suppose that was anxiety, in a nutshell that was it
My therapist would remind me that routine is important
We eat and sleep out of habit more than duty
But you can't always trust habit now can you Ryan
Like one time I watched that very special Ryan
Put all their things in a tidy little box
Then the slow click of the door on its latch
Habit urged me: rise and reach out
But I lay with my head under the duvet
My face got hot with mist
Someone spoke to me, then, from outside the window
As daylight filled the room with silver milk
A small voice I'd been ignoring for a long time

It was the poet Kay Ryan, reminding me that *sometimes*
the green pasture of the mind tilts abruptly
It was Kay Ryan offering me
the greenest saddest strongest kind of hope

In the end, though I'm no movie star, I am also a little attractive
In my own modest way this will always be true
I looked out the window and heard the rain playing
Eternal chopsticks
I thought about this Ryan and that
Felt the name in my mouth, a ragged bell
Inside me something was shimmering
Like a swimming pool at night

)

Neha Maqsood

—

Autumn

Autumn almost always came,
And each time it had a lot to
Tell us.

Of winds harvesting
fields within
the core of the day.
Of trees susurrating
– decreeing that branches
make way.

Days curbed, light waning
as we need it the most.
Leaves,
With disputes of the past burnt
Into them, sloughed off.
An imago.

Dawn sheets the verdures in dew,
Roots take up space in long
Strokes.

Wretched times –
When the past is no longer close.

Like the trace of fog.

A bitch, a live wire

These words are disingenuous.
Lies; like eating within the fringes,
Or perishing before a parent,
Or endeavouring to preclude
The indisputable,
woe.

Not a sin,
Anything but –
to be a woman married to her house.

We cannot promise you anything, but
What us incarcerates have seen within these margins.

To be finished with one's skin and perfumed wrists,

To be seen with child,   )
To be seen without it.

To be woman – binarized. Woman – made
Goldenly from the ribs of man.
Cast up, moulded down.

When will I know how to play my part
In this life. At 12 there was a death of
childhood, when he stroked my hair,
And fastened my headband in the environs.

To feel this intangible dirt on oneself.
The serpent within men.

The world
Never even belonged to us women.

Antosh Wojcik

—

The Local Pit

You are sunburnt
in all our family photos.

In the Texas years
of the album,

we look down on a T-Rex
footprint in a riverbed.

Parents drove us out
to the edge of a canyon.

Probably
a boating lake now –

(

they sell four-flavour
ice cream there.

Back then,
are you thinking jump?

Like you do at the edge
of the local pit,

just around the corner from
where we live?

Fall until your body
is a fossil of light.

A golden wreck
of a boy boating out on you,

drugged on four-flavour
powder cut with ice cream,

hangs a knife up
in your head, 'mistaken'

for a phone. A pit
could be a telephone

for all I know.
I'm calling out to you.

Who's to say you and I
are not the same,

driven to the edge
of some ancient problem.

)

Yolks

A spray-paint death of a man in the middle of the road.
Traffic guided around his outline.

At night, I walk back to him,
curl into the stomach of the drawing.

A dead man's birthmark on the earth.
Everyone wanted you here for longer, I say.

Maybe it feels like a baby kick on the other side.
Maybe he's the lid of heaven.

Pushing my face into the cakey tarmac
I see all sorts of swallowed.

Whole cars with families inside,
songs still fat on the radio.

Dropped fruit and newspapers.
Hail, on pause.

God's barbecuing above the sunken landscape.
We're all trying to be reborn, he says, flipping a burger.

Way, way down, the man who died is still sinking.
The tarmac stretches like yolk.

At home, I fry eggs, the whites
pooling as the dead man's outline.

Egg shells are porous. They pick up all sorts of ideas,
God, dressed as my brother, remarks.

He takes leftovers from the fridge and scuttles off.
The yolk settles in the stomach of the man.

Pan, non-stick like the road.
Everyone wanted you here for longer, I whisper to the egg.

)

Lauren de Sá Naylor
—

In Berlin again, by trans-European train, hanging out in cafés cos the bars are closed (Covid), eating & sipping, very casual.

Decide to hook up with the fam, don't actually ever see them. At first we crawl on hands & knees up an incline, up steps with ever decreasing headroom. Falling plaster, broken structure, like being inside a wall searching for a portal, like being in a staircase labyrinth that proceeds, left-hand always, imperceptibly, so it seems like you're going forward. Someone I trust is behind me & guiding/reassuring me. There is definitely a way out of this.

The place where I'm staying has no privacy & people come/go thru day and night. A man steps into my bed. I can't say no as it seems to be a sharing/boundary-less protocol/space. I try to sleep. Lights on bright. People. Talk. I realise this body beside me will not do. Who are you? How can I tolerate this degree of intimacy? I move my pillow & myself over to the other side of the mattress — top & tail — but of course I then have to contend with his bare feet close to my face.
I just get up & give this up.

(

End up in someone I trust's flat. Recognisable for its gloss red floor. The garden is, like mine, large, concrete, chaotic. As a gift to them? Or is it my purpose here? I decide to clean & sort their things, which are piled up everywhere. I sort the child things from the adult. I don't touch the desk where they work. An antiquated computer screen flashes there, papers & notes. Work. I chop up a life-sized hollow grey humanoid sculpture, I don't understand why.
I know this to be a major transgression. I move on. Details are sparse. Time passes. I'm aware I've gone too far, out of my depth, drowning, interpolating, meddling, pushing, pressing, forcing my way across, through, into. Error. Crashing into your inner sanctum your sacred intimate space with desire desire desire this hunger this desire to be integrated. Meddling does me no favours. It drives you away. A mirror. I know now this feeling of being pursued. To fuck or to hurt me.

Outside with their flatmate, who is a nurse & acquaintance (healer?) talking about the aftermath of my actions. He's wearing a neck brace. They were talking about me last night. Hushed tones of animosity. They're a real bitch you know; I'm glad you did it. My cheeks are burning with shame & regret. What've I done? Ransacking, going forward unrestrained, self-satisfied. Not wanting to be loved, wanting in on something. My dream reflects my life in the reverse and across time. It twists like an infinity band, placing into parallel events/affects from differing times-spaces & perspectives. I miss you I want you I'm sorry I pushed my way in the only thing is time I forgot I didn't know it yet.

*

Hot and close, two or more, black/white checkerboard lino bathroom floor wank, a full house.

Those straight women and their refrain: confusion reigns; & what is heterosexuality anyway, if you hate him & his dick? No dick, no need for it, no need to want it in or on you or to transgress this desire: to be ashamed of wanting it.

A swift fellatio sesh before the train left town, he just knelt down and swallowed it. Man sex. Can't do it like this with women? They don't do it like this: acknowledge a need/express it/be sated. No dates, please. Just let's say what we want/need and decide what we could be for one another.

A young man enters my bar/enters my lucid dream/agency. He's deep-throating my dick, pushing us together, I'm thinking, yeah, he looked at me that way. This, one of my many privileges, has led to one of my many vices. (One way of pulling myself out of bad dream-situations is manufacturing an out-of-body noise that will awaken me. To make the fear 'real'.)

Lift me up, spread my legs, youthful-clumsy-top-bottom-up-thrusting for feeling, knowing the invisible internal membranes of my vulva.

He pressed his leg against hers. Apparently there was no eye contact, which contradicts the witnessed charge (& *eye contact can be too intense*). She pushed my face onto her breasts when I was anxious. Sour sweat was blooming from my armpits, heat was rising, the source of which entwined Dionysus and Apollo in a non-binary desire. A web. Sticky. Awkward. Anxiety plumed from an eros of failure, from error, provoked(!) by a specious proximity-to. Awkwardness. Supremacy. (A pass-agg bollocking coming forthwith.) I dissolved again in a labyrinthine sadness, a low ebb, beating my breast, berating myself. And slept none.

It was the myth/night of the young man dream. Lucid. Held between conscious and unconscious pillars, seated like The Priestess, regal and yet protecting some bodily aspect. Super-emphasis on harshness of body affect, the hustle and limits.

*

My mother told me – you look like a nun with your keys hanging round your neck. You look like my mother; she always wore a collared blouse or a shirt-dress. With your check shirt, you look like you, as a teenager.

Between nun & mother & teen, there's a truth that persists. Something about the denial of the body. Of obfuscating femininity & sequestering sexuality. At least, adjusting its coordinates, rendering it illegible to most. Keeping it personal, close, enclosed. Something about flesh, crisis & shame. Something about self-denial & pushing out to the margins. Something auto-erotic, self-sufficient, in service to the self. These foundations of an *erotics of sharing*.

But *I'm* nothing like a nun! To which my mother argued: well, how do you know, you don't know what they get up to. Resounding yes. Similar types of embodiment & refusal? Well, of course, and she would know more than me – convent educated in Latin America. Even the British sixth-form college was Catholic. No icons at home. We're all made in refusal/denial.

Both my grandmothers favoured the button-down shirt, the collared blouse. The backwards garment, revealing not *décolletage* but nape and back. *Far more becoming for a woman of my age.* Sexier at any age. Another, subtle exposure of flesh. Not thigh or bust, though they are conspicuous by their 'absence', but ankle, wrist, foot, neck.

Unlike the nun. Cloaked. *Cloaca is the posterior orifice that serves as the only opening for the digestive, reproductive and urinary tracts of many vertebrate animals. Cloaca* is Latin for sewer. The cloaca is hidden. Being hooded is a biological fact of socially constructed womanliness that also mirrors, mimics. Mirrors this anatomy that burrows into as opposed to springs out of the groin. I never really thought of this negatory genitalia as less, or a void, more as a vessel, a cup. A generative space, a cavern, a chamber, something with serious walls. Something upon which space is *predicated*.

 Did I really think that? Rarely did I go inside. Somehow knowing the fallacy of penetration. Intuiting, via fear of penetration, that surfaces have depths.

 I was proud to remind my mother of the nuns who schooled her in that Brazilian convent. And, like the grandmothers, wearing their shirts. (Some nights I ponder the cloistered life.) In my mother's imaginal fellowship of these disparate females, she reveals some underlying sense of what my body is. This covered, unkempt, gnawed.

 This familiar flavour of femininity that refuses submission or legibility, passing-over meek & mildness, side-swerving drag, discarding the playfulness of dress-up, not quite measuring up, dialing-down.

 I watched Jasmine and Jude and I understood; I carry womanhood *as such*, my big-dick energy is feminine, and yet I'm battling it. As when a medical intervention intersected with my lover's desire, it rendered my body a battleground. And with Nwando, talking pampering practices, service work, and the affect brought about by acrylic nails, I started to wonder: have I become, like the discourse, averse to qualities that in (other) 'women' I do admire?

)

Astra Papachristodoulou
—
Apis Tentacular

(

this long overcrowding   portions of layers   whole layers and unknowing

the harmony of overwhelming and collective murder

i am not there to interrupt

bees drawn along   and rough   and along

this is the sign of new death

Astra Papachristodoulou

(

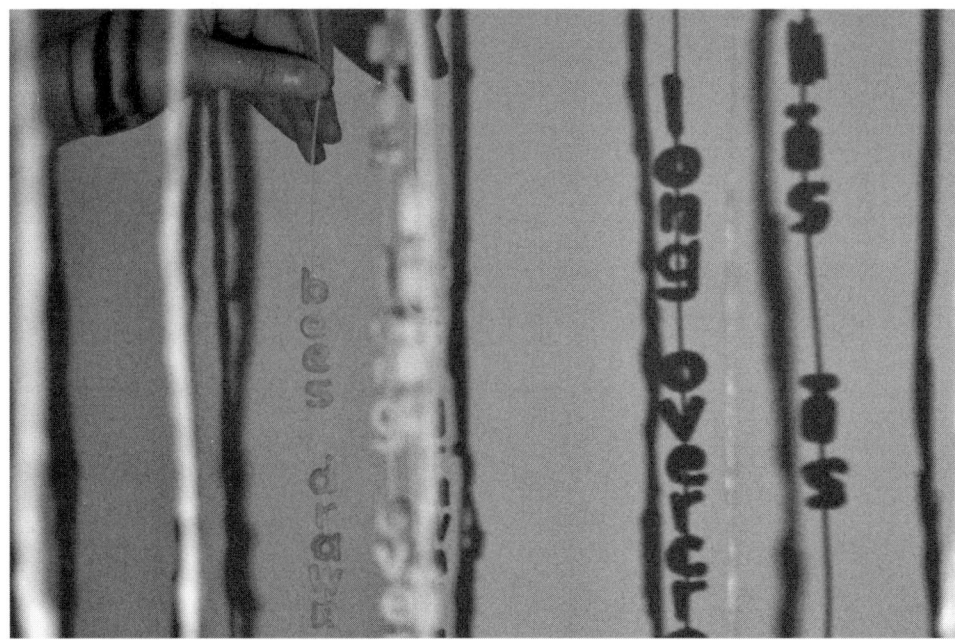

Eric Langley & James Gaywood

—

Pathlines

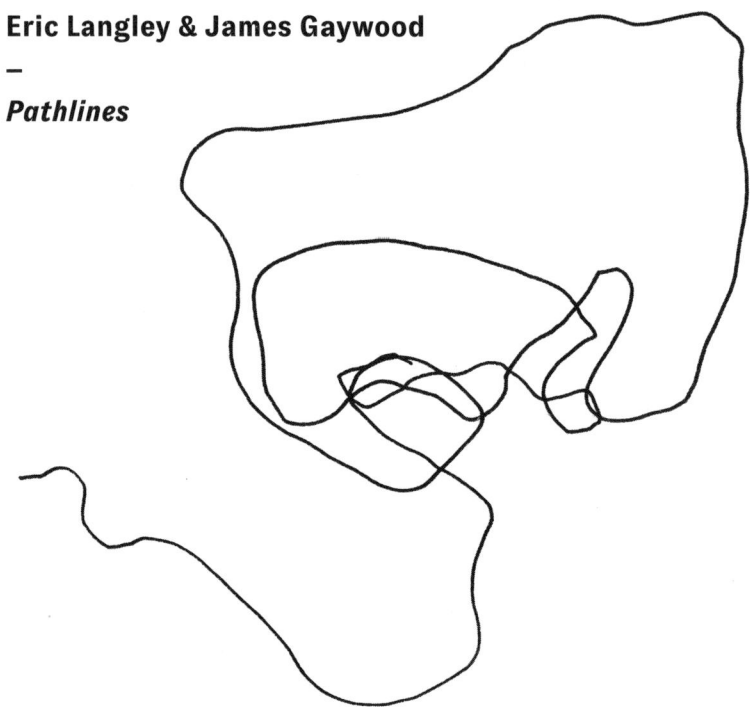

(
    Friday evening, ten-past nine, with darkness
        coming on   – here as now –   while cloud covers
and low light lengthens-out its interests
   – rose & golden – in the here & now around us:
situated   in our distinct darkness,
    cute to some sharp centre-pip – spot-lit –
    fine at the focal point of dim dispersal,
      we take up our precise placement,   and are
        adopted in the dusk,   accordingly.

      Accordingly, by all deft account and
      in relation.   Addressing each memory,
lipped out   on the glance & backdraft, and tipped
      towards us, in expectancy, as swifts
            swoon up,
            soft on an
                updraft,
              cycling.

Pathline I: Swift, *Apus apus*, 07/20

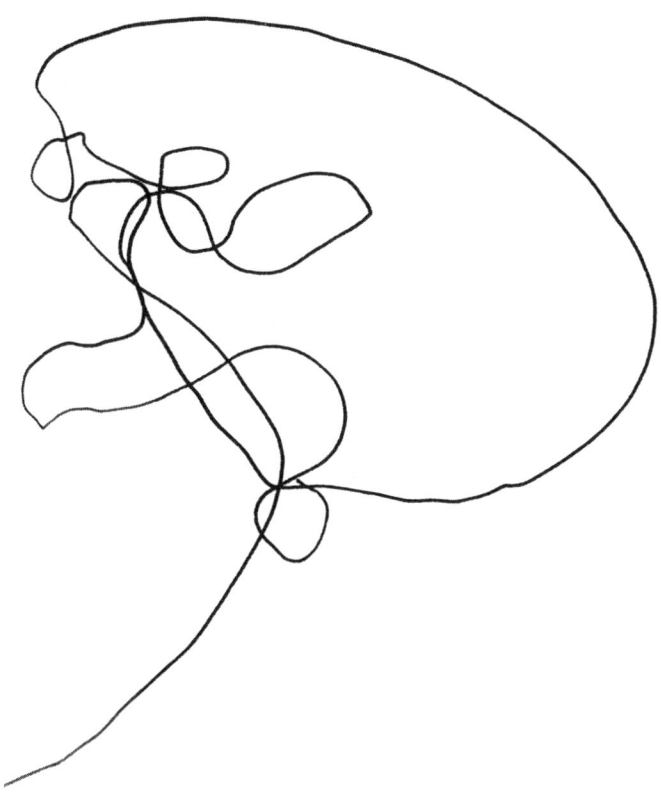

)

They spot *us*, slo-mo, fixed from 10,000 ft:
(*lost*) object-oriented in each approach.
                Out in ecstasies of it.
              Ecstasies.

      Your eye is set (*ecstatic*) on their cool vanishing;
        your flat pad leadline traces tracks, and out (*ecstatic*)
  along   across   among a fluid fine-line,
            lacing horizontal complexity,
        perplexing its lateral interface,
          implying implicated depths, deft-drawn,
       describing distance, and O involving
              volumes of it.   So you're beside yourself!
    & circling, circling,   extravagantly.

    You stretched-out (then) to sound-at each & every
plumb-plumed depth o' them: hyperbolic tangles.

Pathline II: Swift, *Apus apus*, 07/20

Eric Langley & James Gaywood

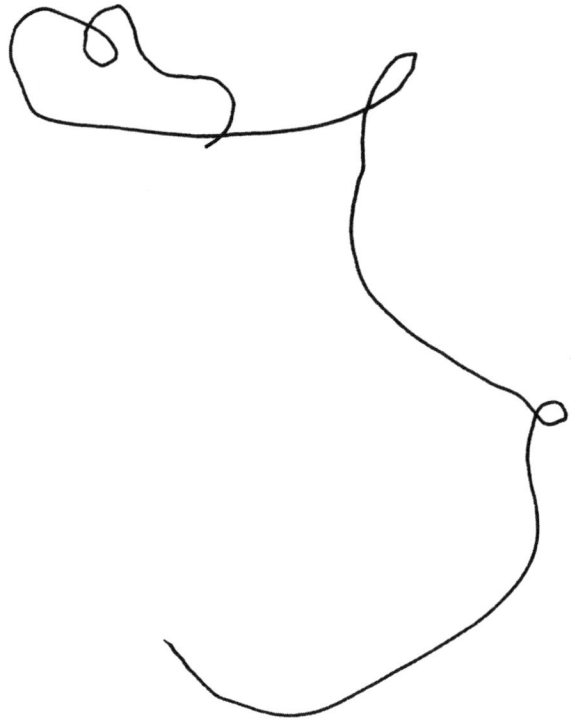

(

Out, sat saturate, among the branchlines,
        sliding in around the slowcurve, or in
among the sharper swerves, edge cut or jagged
-back cutely.   Or, just momentarily,
       bound in, loosely, to a bumbling, hectic
     spirograph of less abrupt diversions,
               lost attentions, warm wanderings in some
     softspun jumble.   Do the drone thing, lazily.

Above us, wonderblue.   And through the blue,
    swifts thread tracerfire,   all scream & soaring
-out from *swipt*, from *sweep*, from *swip*, *sweep*, & *swive*;
        happy in all their etymologies.

So high now that the overhead opens,
                    canopies
              out-and-up, enormously.

Pathline III: Swift, *Apus apus*, 07/20

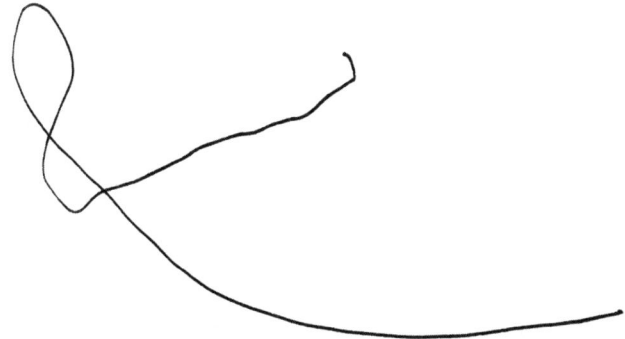

From one fixed point in the stupendous whole
    every switch-up cuts cute perplexity,
  slips back spiralised in cones of heat-rise
    etching such a hectic helix, in loops
           haphazard, on a deep-green ferric sky.

      Intaglio in the azure blue and
sweeping, clean across the skyblue scatter.

Each enacted turn is a bone-twitch from
        the wingtip's sudden flinch & triggerpinch,
     jagged off into a steely cool skyplate,
  as biting breaks sharp or smooth & curling
    purls of warm wax, furred from the tacky ground.

Dipped in mordant, each bird flips chloride spit,
    as nitric flicks spit sheer from feathertip.

Pathline IV: Swift, *Apus apus*, 07/20

Eric Langley & James Gaywood

(

Catch them as they come, careening, spattering
    the sky in twists of turpentine.   Airborne.

    These two-dimensional ink impressions
– *flat-pack their private intricate pathways;*
        snatch such confidential cartographies –
record much deeper divings, depths of them,
speaking of the soar the scream, & wheeling
        stratospheric, gone up in ascendence.

    Oriented by their meandering paths,
you wait, tucked to the turnstiles, patient, for
        some unforeseen signature, all on the
    off-chance.   Go hold out your ring-bound note-pad;
    your hopeful spirograph, rolling round, and
up for it.   Extortion by etch-a-sketch.

Catch at them as they come, creamed in their career,
    slicing sharp autographs on your eyeline.

Pathline V: Swift, *Apus apus*, 07/20

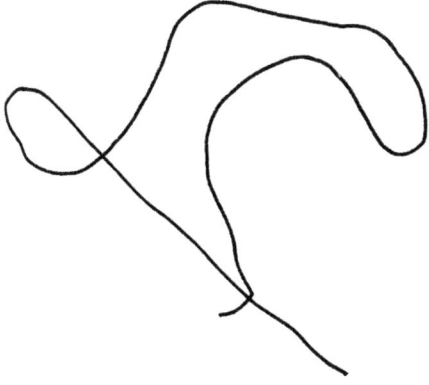

    Now, herring-gulls sling out far flung and low
        to landscape, implacable in business.   )

    Carrion crows mark each edge of what we know.

                Illegible skyline scriptures sign off
                investment opportunities, lost in
  our thinner dusk.   Such stranged signatures, scrawled
    cryptically right at the peripheries
of our eyeline;   placed perhaps just before
    our recent search histories,   just beyond.

    As crows fly, right across the pantomime.

Opt out of each amazing intricate interlace
    as you see fit, claiming your independence;
       you're left, nervous in the dark, tonight;
          woken, restless, to the cries of gulls,   mocking you.

Pathline VI: Herring gull, *Larus argentatus*, 09/20

Edwina Attlee

—

January

How wet your trumpets are
under golden leaves
five little coughs arranged around the forehead
like a halo

(

February

A ballet in the snow
he lifts the axe to chop the wood
prances across the yard

the crows eat up the corn
the baby is back
and the women open their legs to the stove
pushing soft porridge into his mouth
like *companionable silence*

outside
a well-thatched fence
bee hives topped with snow
smoke pooping from a little chimney

into a very bleak sky.

               Toil in the corner of the Book of Hours
               includes sewing, small eyes, hard hands made brittle   )
               by the hand of the artist who must know hands.
               Toil raking the rake
               through the soil, it too is brittle
               I have planted too many seeds
               forgot not to work every hour
               plunging little white shoots into
               velvety ground. It was good pushing the seeds down
               but now they are uncomfortable
               and crowded
               like the lumpy pillow in the single bed
               where you sometimes make me sleep
               and where the mice run scuttle through the walls.

This month I find myself unwittingly open
to the church and the field you dragged in
air like starch under the skirt
your large hands red as dust
your swollen sense of being
rightly granted the right to all of us
and our hours.

March

They call this sewing
the bad stumps need to be pulled up
the rivets made real
new potatoes and roots pushed down.
The cattle make for lighter work
the black one looks like the pale one's shadow
that ground is untidy.
Hard not to wish for order
or that the mud would solve itself
grow backwards grow rich
we work in the shadow of the castle
we work alone

the men come   they smell of roses
a stench that reminds me how old I am
and how I fail

(

my sister burns her papers in the stove
makes plans to leave
I watch in silence   I would have
the words to rescue her
the colour to mop up
some of the blood
the blood moon
pooling in her bowl
night after night she finds it

In my dreams we travel together
I have some money   we visit
the abortion clinic   the refuge   the housing estate
I hold her elbow lightly
try to see what she's seeing
observe the prohibition against photographs

in the estate
a little scooped out place
like Henry Moore's ladies' elbows
soft as body hair
she tells me she dreams about suicide
I am squeezed by memory
the little coin slipping like liquid between the pressing parts
coming out *stamped* and shamefaced
hot hands uncovered sorry
memory conscious of its begetting
cheapens it
afraid of noticing how
tender how
dear
your news is bad
I am pierced
they call this sewing
the price of soft hands
and softened fabric   I pat her gloves with foam   )
blow bubbles in the dusk
with liquid from the pound shop
she wants to leave
she wants to grow somewhere else like a
packet of seeds
I want to bash her all over
with a frying panhammer
like this moment which has already got away
and which I forbid you to talk about
no poem   no hymn
do it without the commentary
alone or in silence
on a walk in the tube

I have an hour to tell you
I love you   this bluely
your body   is a hot peach
your mind   a foot stepping over   a brook
the unseen   gallant   pageboy   stepping
his high steps   I falter   in your orange
arrowroot   burning paper   dark undarking
gold tooth   every wish
every plan   every moan
you are a great shaking precedent
a headrest in marble   a saint uplit upon the pillow
your selfishness
leaves you undiminished and brutal

(I can see everything
you will go far away
just remember
I found you at the high table
and felt so small and surprised

(from *Book of Days*)

Campbell Andersen

—

Spread

I do not raise the question. It is out there already, unsaid and projected, hanging over the two of us in the dusk. The air is heavy. There is some kind of ribbon or string moving in the hot wind, caught on the wire above the side fencing of the yard. From some old helium balloon maybe, released in celebration or by clumsy grip. Ali is quiet, his head between his legs. He has rolled up one leg of his jeans to give air to a healing calf tattoo. We talk about the permanence of ink on the largest human organ; shapes and figures and meaningless symbols. We talk about dead languages, ancient hieroglyphs, cave markings. The halogen light above us is brilliant and constant, humming loudly; bugs and insects make random fleeting shadows on the gravel yard, and out beyond the light are beat-up cars and vehicles, here with dings and scrapes and scratches. Write-offs and complete repairs. All this depending on the severity of what has been done. The question is simple enough that it could really be implied. How Ali is feeling is just the first layer; I am yet to unveil the damage done, spread. The full volume of distribution.

We talk around the question; on and about energy and fatigue. About sex, average sex, libido and drive, awkward stilted sex. We talk about terrorism, attacks on the West, primary instigators, figures; places and names, casualties, faulty wiring. The effectiveness of smoke detectors. Larger topics are skirted and skimmed, acting as set-ups or prologues to smaller moments, subject-matter concerning occupations and careers, the banal lives of production workers, fast-food service professionals, men and women who euthanise animals and healthcare workers who provide palliative care. We go quiet and listen to the hushed dying sounds of day. Cars pass on the street adjacent. Ali picks up on the thunder-crack of a Yamaha MT-07 way off inside the residential area, several streets away. He states the make and model of the motorcycle, but that is all. Nothing on how he knows what it sounds like, and nothing about particular characteristics, indicators, signifiers that provide context or prior knowledge. He simply says it and it is real. A kind of vague truth.

We are seated on the second step of the staircase external to the building, leading up to the warehouse office. The steps themselves are made of galvanised steel. They are ribbed, uncomfortable. Manufactured for shoes, boots, feet in general; so sitting on them feels strangely wrong. Ali has finished a can of Sprite and is gradually loosening the ring tab off the top. He does it carefully, with purpose and aim, his face a blank sheet and his focus elsewhere. The quiet takes us over, becomes everything in one moment, and we decide to talk again, breaking silence with words and cues. We talk about soft drinks and energy drinks, alcohol and narcotics. Sugar content, dietary fibre, our favourite breakfast cereals. About the fact that there is an answer for every question, verbalised or not. Answers taking many forms but questions being unified and patterned, easy enough to gauge and understand. A want for more content; some questions as necessities, others acting as desperate desire for explanation. Gaps in information.

Somehow our talk is funneled down, narrowed and hemmed. We talk about analgesics, cytotoxic drugs. Breakthrough pain and pain relief. We are resigned to foreign medical speech that we know little about. Words like metastasise and sarcoma. Like lymph. We talk about cures, venoms and antidotes. Physiological reactions, mortality rates and life expectancy. Ali speaks of a man in Szechuan who lived to 256. We talk about extreme longevity, myth, legend and rumour. The propulsive authority of the Internet. Often our words are stunted, short. Ali pronounces 'engine' like 'injun', something I absorb but do not mention. We watch shadows at the edge of the floodlight's perimeter and laugh at a graffitied Nissan at the rear of the yard, lit up by passing headlights, tagged in pink and white with the words SORRY ABOUT YOUR CAR. We laugh and it's good for a while. We talk about money and wallets. The multiple uses of cow leather. Waterproofing, water-resistance, precipitation and rain. Shifts in temperature extremes, late monsoon onset, increased fire danger. We feel small and molecular, everything around us prickled and feverish.

The wind is warm and strong. The ribbon on the wire fencing is lifted and suppressed without control, snagged and wrapped, lapping tide-like against itself. It is another piece, a pixel within the scene we are in, its meaning attributed through our collective lens. Filtered through each of us. Ali has taken the ring tab off his can and is imprinting the aluminium shape of it into the pad of his finger. There is capillary retention and release, his brown skin briefly dented and then smoothed. The sounds of crinkled confectionery wrappers in the street gutters, bleating horns, crickets and cicadas, moths fizzing at the white glare. There are the sounds of trees and the tap of a flagpole's halyard. Things moving against themselves, against their own grains and fibres. Noises of me swallowing; workings of the inner ear. We do not speak when Ali flings the ring tab across the gravel and there is no talk too when we hear the squealing rip of rubber and the collision of two vehicles outside on the street.

The accident occurs in full vision. Our view from the metal stair is prime, front-row. A small sedan, something of Korean make, is squeezed between a parked Jeep and a four-wheel drive travelling the same way as the sedan, east, the sedan hinged up on two wheels and the four-wheel drive out in front. The whip of clanged metal. Broken window glass, a brief asphalt scrape. The small grey Korean car's hazard lights blink on and off through the lingering smoke of the accident, its underside – its important working belly – exposed and darkly hot. The sound itself does not match the seriousness of the collision. Disparity in noise and action, like a nuke's distant shockwave, kilometres of flattened earth. Shattered home windows in neighbouring cities, unheard and unfelt until minutes after impact. What is seen in reality is the sedan's quite gentle upending and fall onto its side. As if the car had fainted or stumbled drunk. With the scene more or less dark, people moving around are pictures, silhouettes, the bright red of the four-wheel drive's brake lights parked on the road just out of sight, an orange streetlight dousing the asphalt with dim visual aid. There are accusatory voices, intonations, surrendered hands thrown up above shoulders. They are attempting to establish not how the accident occurred but who is in the wrong.

Within the floodlight's boundary, Ali and I feel impartial, neutral to the accident. We are content with watching things unfold, seeing this strange happening for what it is without breaching the line between the two parties. We speculate names and occupations of the silhouettes, attributing personalities and characteristics to voices, clear and complete and unknown in the night. The night just beginning. A jolting black and the breeze cooling, and the bickering voices dying down now, willing to forgive and thank God that everyone is whole and well. We talk about blame, the innate want to shift or palm off responsibility. Softly, under the murmured discussions between the drivers on the street, we talk about time. Minutes, hours, days. Staggered fragments of equal length. We return to the question like it is some guiding pole, a narrative symbol which we base all other talk around. The question of how much time, the question based on spread, malignancy. I pick at a hangnail with my teeth. Ali observes the scene playing out on the street. He says they are both wrong, both drivers. I ask him why, but he doesn't answer; remaining quiet affords him a kind of mystery. It is not a need but a wish to understand him; it goes deeper than conversation.

There are other bystanders collecting at the edges of the accident. Flashes of phone torchlights, extra voices. Someone has called it in. Then with the muted sounds of sirens, I imagine the blue-red flashing lights of the ambulance. This is his future; in some respect this will be his moment of death. Culmination of X-rays and consultations and estimated timeframes. The pure breadth of doctors, oncologists. I think about Ali's thick Eastern hair coming out in thready chunks. This mass of veins and arterial pushing, narrowing, limited on those final hours into four white walls and a plaid bed that is white as well, a bed that is adjustable and has legs that fold into itself, a bed that has had so many other people atop it. They would say that this is a perfectly normal reaction, essential hysteria and paranoia a natural part of the grieving process. A five-stage, five-letter acronym to help you remember. I hear the sirens coming, louder. And though I know they are not, I feel they are coming for him, to take him peacefully into more white places in which, after much effort and acceptance, he will not resist.

(This story was shortlisted for the Desperate Literature Prize for Short Fiction 2021, for which *PROTOTYPE* was a partner journal.)

Yuri Felsen
trans. Bryan Karetnyk
—
Extras

Throughout the last decade of the Russian émigré writer Yuri Felsen's life (1894–1943), his creative energies were consumed by a major literary venture titled The Recurrence of Things Past. *Encompassing three novels as well as seven interlinking novellas and short stories by his untimely death in 1943, the project was conceived of as an ever-evolving 'human document'. Its narrative unfolds episodically, jigsaw-like, revealing a composite psychological portrait of the narrator Volodya, a neurasthenic and aspiring author, whose thwarted amorous pursuits generate beautifully wrought extemporisations on love, literature and human nature. In this episode, 'Extras', the dreamy protagonist, addressing his prose, as ever, to his cruel and fickle muse, recounts a trip to a film studio on the outskirts of Paris. Even in Felsen's day, the extra, the 'background artist', had become emblematic of the very condition of exile. Here, however, Felsen takes this anonymous, voiceless mass of 'human shame' and individualises it, distinguishing the private histories of those whom chance has reduced to playing the obscurest of parts. This fragment of his great* roman inachevé *shines a small spotlight on his work, allowing him a brief cameo in advance of his starring role. Felsen's first novel,* Deceit, *will be published by Prototype in 2022.*

( )

Petrik, my dearest friend, recently offered to fix me up as an extra on a film-shoot. Not without some embarrassment did I accept his offer, knowing full well that it would mean degrading myself, capitulating somehow in life's struggle, since I should be obliged to settle for the sorriest part in it. Petrik gave me all the necessary details—I was to travel out of town to some remote studio, where I was to mention his name. I should have to get up at some ungodly hour, with the disagreeable prospect of impending boredom and shame, of dissolution in some shabby, squalid crowd. As I made my way to the outskirts of town on that wretched tram, I began sizing up the dubious-looking, excessively made-up, elegant young things with tired, bleary eyes, the unshaven men straight from a night in Montmartre, the bright-eyed, boisterous Russian Parisians of average height and exceptionally rakish, cavalier, idle disposition—and in them I identified unmistakable 'comrades in misfortune', otherwise known as my immediate competitors. I even feared that I might have to make the return journey empty-handed, without the requisite cash, without hope of any further (albeit modest) remuneration, and that Petrik would reproach me for everything, as he had once done Pavlik for his ineptitude and indolence.

Alighting the tram after the others, I followed them down country lanes and muddy district roads, across a square with a monument to the war dead (a stone angel and a soldier with a rifle and helmet), along a quiet, well-tended cemetery (the kind that allays the very fear of death), until we all of us arrived at a vast, gloomy, barn-like affair crammed full of people. Having satisfied myself that 'the management' had yet to appear, I took a seat on a bench and buried myself in a Russian book, trying not to let my eyes rove.

'You're Russian? Pleased to meet you. What's that you're reading? *Oh-lye-sha*? Never heard of him.' I was afforded a certain sense of relief by this introduction, with its show of conviviality, so necessary in these situations, and engaged in friendly conversation this portly, round-faced, elderly little gentleman, who was wearing a pince-nez and smoking a pipe with an impossibly long stem. He turned out to be a lawyer from Petersburg and, having stumbled upon a 'fellow countryman', began recalling fondly the Petersburg theatres, the names of the streets, the numbers and routes of the trams, the *gymnasium*, the university, the professors—everything that could wrest us both from these degrading circumstances. 'There are so few respectable people around here,' he said, and, as though to stress that I numbered among those rare exceptions, he introduced me to his wife, a stout, dark-browed lady who wore on her snub-nosed, soft, kind Slavic face an expression of grandeur mingled with apprehension. 'And this is my friend, the Baron Dehm, cavalry.' The Baron, a tall, stooping gentleman with a pendulous, bushy ginger moustache, bowed to me gravely and with indifference, maintaining his phlegmatic silence. The little lawyer, on the other hand, was exceedingly talkative and amiable; wishing to justify, as it were, his presence in this clearly abject situation, he explained to me, with feigned bravado and nonchalance, that he had lost 'a heap of money' on the stock market, that he would soon 'land something lucrative', but that until then he would have to get by however he could: 'The wife and I need to make a thousand a week at the very least.' He was ashamed even for his friend. 'The Baron has a wealthy brother and sister in London, but, alas, he squanders every last penny he has on drink,' he said, before adding unexpectedly, in a rapid whisper: 'He and I met on the front, though I myself am no guardsman. I joined the ranks on principle, much to the consternation of my illustrious relations—my family name, Ivanov, is common enough, although my ancestors were princes of the realm. But then who cares about such things now?'

As he was talking, a subtle commotion erupted almost imperceptibly; everybody stirred, many got to their feet, as though preparing for some decisive action—at last 'the management' had arrived, along with a swarthy-looking young lady who moved quickly and unnaturally on dumpy legs: 'That's their secretary, Mademoiselle Klein—a Jewess, but a decent sort and pleasant enough.' Having removed her mackintosh and beret as she went, she ducked into a ramshackle little room with rough wooden walls that, to all appearances, had been knocked together in great haste; a dozen gaily-coloured posters covered some tattered wallpaper and there was an inscription over the door: Bureaux. A line of extras, chiefly Russians, stretched out outside it, and I, smiling the entreating smile of the herd, gave my name and alluded to Petrik's recommendation. Without looking up from the open file in front of her, Mademoiselle Klein lazily intoned the well-rehearsed line: 'Wait here. You'll be called soon.' Then, like generals on parade, a separate, glittering group strode past: the directors and chief assistants, among them Bobby in a crisply pressed suit—he was not in the least surprised to see me and whispered condescendingly as he passed: 'Don't let on that you know me. It won't do you any favours.' I sensed that he was afraid of discrediting himself with a compromising acquaintance, but I did not begrudge him this and was even glad of his undoubtedly advantageous advice. My companion suddenly leapt to his feet and ran over to a swarthy, grey-haired, dignified-looking gentleman—judging by his austere air and demeanour, the most important figure of all—and this latter, with artificial though impeccable manners, shook his hand firmly and led him into the office. From there the little lawyer returned happy, but suddenly checked himself and with a businesslike indifference declared: 'An old colleague. We speculated together in Berlin. What can I say? He's had a bit of luck here. A pity I didn't manage to introduce my wife, but then again, he did invite us both to drop in on him.' And, turning to her, again with that beaming face: 'To think, what a strange coincidence.' I instinctively compared this courteous grey-haired director to Bobby and ascribed Bobby's cold-blooded betrayal to the unfounded, uncalled-for, unscrupulous (in matters of money), barefaced careerism of his (and thus my) generation. In all likelihood, this 'old colleague' was no better, no more or less decent than Bobby, but at least he maintained a veneer of civility; more and more I value those old 'pharisaic' conventions that we have lost, that outward form of discourse at which we used to poke so much fun but which eased its very essence—rather like those do-gooding handouts that stave off hunger. As I observed Bobby and his pompous, imperious ways, I recalled Mannie Davydov's suggestion that I become his secretary and my refusal at the time: had I acquiesced, I should number today among 'the management' and Bobby would not have been ashamed to be seen with me. I do not regret it, though: in taking the job intended for Pavlik, I should have broken your many years of trust in me and lost you forever.

As they scrambled over one another, these thoughts of mine were interrupted by Mademoiselle Klein, who was hurriedly calling us (out of turn, Ivanov and his wife taking priority); we were given some sort of ticket and dispatched to a stark new barracks-like structure that was damp and cold and to my mind resembled a disused village theatre. The renowned Russian director, wearing a markedly casual, unseasonably bright jacket, a man of average height and pasty countenance, fat and bald, with great, morose, bugling eyes, stood somehow helplessly before us, giving instructions to his nearest assistants and technicians (all dressed in caps and apache neckerchiefs, as if to spite their well-heeled, dapper *patrons*).

One by one, we were arranged in a ludicrously haphazard order, and I was struck—although I had the vague notion of this even earlier—by the conceited despondency of the men and the energetic, airy, affected coquetry of the women (two friends, for example, both elegant, made-up Russian ladies, spent the whole time gadding about arm-in-arm, not wanting to be separated on the *plateau*—which the director indulgently allowed): evidently, many of them, having been fed on a diet of industry advertising about pictures and '*vedettes*', had come here in the hope of success, with the intention of making their debuts and, having spontaneously, magnificently dazzled whomever necessary, winning fame. In the given instance, however, none of this was possible: everything required of us was much too simple and uninspired—we had to play happy English countryfolk welcoming the king and his young wife with joyous cries ('Long live the King!' and 'She loves him, loves him!'). As we did this, the two young Russian ladies in the front row, with exaggerated English accents, vociferated their enthusiasm, which bordered on frenzy; their efforts, needless to say, went unnoticed. I was surprised by the Ivanovs' work ethic, shouting as they did with a kind of spirited desperation and that inimitable Russian pronunciation—only the Baron gave a sullen and disdainful sniff as he maintained his silence.

They let us go for lunch and dinner—in some dingy 'bistro' we drank ghastly coffee and ate sandwiches topped with some insipid cured ham. I was suddenly taken by an urge to economise and not waste a penny of my 'fee', as though work and play were two separate arenas, and where business reigns, one must be thrifty. As always, there were amusing incidents that one could never have dreamt up—over lunch, not far from me, a Russian lady was putting on youthful airs and complaining as she touched up her lips: 'Nobody understands my suffering; they've all got it in for me. What sort of a life is this?'

We wasted a whole day and half the night on our undemanding programme, then—having pocketed our lavish pay—we were dispatched back to the city aboard creaking trucks, like soldiers, and I, as behoves a third-rate businessman, spent the journey reckoning the unprofitability of 'their' enterprise. We all had to sit and wait for the first métro in a dubious-looking café on the outskirts of town, while fat little Ivanov, aglow with success, reminisced interminably about cavalry charges, shrapnel fire and titled *aides-de-camp*, although the weary, grim Baron could not bestir himself, and his prosaic, distinctly plebeian wife talked ecstatically of the remarkable encounter with the director, of fate, of 'terms' and of money. Before, in pre-émigré, 'normal' times, I dare say such a meeting of two old friends, under such circumstances and in such a setting, would have seemed extraordinarily romantic, but everything has changed so much in exile, the higher-ups are within reach of the lower-downs, so fragile are names, status and wealth that it was not, for instance, the singularity, the unexpectedness of the encounter that aroused the astonishment of Ivanov's wife; in truth, she experienced nothing but envy, resentment towards her husband, and the hope for some additional favour.

(

CONTRIBUTOR BIOGRAPHIES

Rachael Allen is the author of *Kingdomland* (Faber) and co-author of numerous artists' books, including *Nights of Poor Sleep* (Test Centre), *Almost One*, *Say Again!* (Slimvolume) and *Green at an Angle* (Kestle Barton). She was recently Anthony Burgess Fellow at the University of Manchester, and is the poetry editor for Granta magazine and books.

Campbell Andersen received his Bachelor of Arts in Creative Writing from RMIT. Based in Melbourne, Australia, he writes short fiction about identity, anxiety and the weirdness of modern life. He remains intensely interested in the way we communicate and connect as human beings.

Edwina Attlee is the author of two pamphlets of poetry, *the cream* (Clinic, 2016) and *Roasting Baby* (If A Leaf Falls Press, 2016). Her writing has also appeared in *McSweeney's*, *The People' House*, *Try To Be Better* and *Test Centre 8*.

Rowland Bagnall's first collection, *A Few Interiors*, was published by Carcanet in 2019. He is currently working towards a PhD in Creative Writing at the University of Birmingham. More work and information can be found at www.rowlandbagnall.com.

Tom Betteridge is a writer and researcher living in London. He is the author of the poetry pamphlets *Mudchute* (forthcoming from Veer, 2021), *Dressings* (MATERIALS, 2019), *Body Work* (Sad Press, 2018) and *Pedicure* (sine wave peak, 2017). With Dr Ellen Dillon he co-edited *The Journal of British and Irish Innovative Poetry*'s special issue on Peter Manson's poetry and translations.

Sam Buchan-Watts is the author of *Faber New Poets 15* and co-editor, with Lavinia Singer, of *Try To Be Better* (Prototype, 2019), a creative-critical engagement with W. S. Graham. In 2018 he undertook a fellowship at the Yale Center for British Art. He is the recipient of an Eric Gregory Award (2016) and a Northern Writers' Award for Poetry (2019). His debut collection, *Path Through Wood*, is forthcoming from Prototype in October 2021.

Pavel Büchler is an artist living in Manchester.

Paul Buck has been writing and publishing since the late Sixties. His work is characterised by its sabotaging of the various forms in order to explore their overlaps and differences. Through the Seventies he also edited the seminal magazine *Curtains*, with its focus on threading French writing from Bataille, Blanchot, Jabès, Faye, Noël, Ronat, Collobert and a score of others into a weave with English and American writers and artists. While editing and translating are still a daily activity – in partnership with Catherine Petit, the Vauxhall&Company series of books at Cabinet Gallery is their responsibility – he also continues to cover new ground: *Spread Wide*, a fiction generated from his letters with Kathy Acker; *A Public Intimacy*, strip-searching scrapbooks to expose autobiography; *Disappearing Curtains*, an exhibition catalogue that collides with a 'journal'; *Library: a suitable case for treatment*, a collection of essays. In 2019 he helped Laure Prouvost to write her film *Deep See Blue Surrounding You*, around which her Venice Biennale pavilion, representing France, was based. Most recently he has published the narratives *Indiscretions* (*& Nakedness*) with Vauxhall&Company, further essays, *Street of Dreams*, with Ma Bibliothèque, and his novel *Along the River Run* with Prototype.

Theodoros Chiotis has published the chapbooks *Screen* (Paper Tigers Books, 2017) and *limit.less: towards an assembly of the sick* (Litmus, 2017). He is also the editor and translator of the anthology *Futures: Poetry of the Greek Crisis* (Penned in the Margins, 2015). His work has been published in *Litmus*, *Datableed*, *Forward Book of Poetry 2017*, *3:AM Magazine*, *Adventures in Form*, *Shearsman*, amongst others. He has received awards and commendations from the Forward Arts Foundation and the Institute for the Future of the Book. He is on the editorial board of *[φρμκ]* and of *Hotel* magazine. He currently lives and works in Athens.

Natalie Crick (Newcastle, UK) has had poems published in *Stand*, *The Moth*, *Banshee*, *The Dark Horse*, *The Poetry Review*, *New Welsh Review* and elsewhere. She is studying for an MPhil in Creative Writing at Newcastle University. Last year one of Natalie's poems was commended in the Verve Poetry Festival Competition 2020 and awarded second prize in the Newcastle Poetry Competition 2020. One of her poems received a special mention by judge Ilya Kaminsky in the Poetry London Prize 2020. This year a poem was highly commended in the Folklore Poetry Prize, highly commended in the Wales Poetry Award and she received a nomination for The Forward Prize for Best Single Poem.

CONTRIBUTOR BIOGRAPHIES

Raluca de Soleil is a multidisciplinary artist working across poetry, photography, video, performance and abstract painting. Her debut poetry collection *Adulthood is a lifelong conversation about what we used to do as kids*, explores early-life disconnection, its causes and consequences. Raluca aims to create a space for emotional honesty, acknowledging personal-political trauma and discovering alternatives to the oppressive structures inhabiting and inhibiting our minds.

Roisin Dunnett's fiction has appeared in *Ambit*, *Hotel* and elsewhere. She is currently undertaking an MA in Creative and Life Writing at Goldsmiths. Her debut fiction pamphlet, *Animal, Vegetable*, is published by Broken Sleep Books.

Maia Elsner's debut collection, *overrun by wild boars*, will be published by flipped eye in July 2021. Recently, her work has appeared in *Magma*, *Poetry Ireland* and *The Maine Review*. The poems included in this anthology are part of an ekphrastic sequence inspired by her paternal grandfather, who was a Holocaust survivor and found in painting and pottery a reason for hope after so much loss. She is currently working on a poetry-film collaboration project, and on translating Latin American writers into English.

Yuri Felsen is the pen name of Nikolai Freudenstein (1894–1943), who was born in St Petersburg and emigrated to Paris in the wake of the October Revolution of 1917. Held to be one of the most innovative and important writers of his generation alongside Vladimir Nabokov, he fell into obscurity after his death at Auschwitz, and his work is only now being translated into English.

SJ Fowler is a writer, poet and artist who lives in London. His writing has explored subjects as diverse as prescription drugs, films, fight sports, museums, prisons and animals and his work has been commissioned by Tate Modern, BBC Radio 3, Somerset House, Tate Britain, the National Centre for Writing and the National Poetry Library amongst others. He's been translated into 27 languages and produced collaborations with over 150 artists. He has pioneered the fields of performance literature, literary curation, visual, photo and film poetry, collaborative poetry and Neuropoetics. stevenjfowler.com

Ella Frears is a poet and artist based in London. Her debut collection *Shine, Darling* (Offord Road Books, 2020) was shortlisted for both the Forward Prize for Best First Collection and the T. S. Eliot Prize for Poetry.

Sam Fuller has been published in several poetry collections and he won the Projector Poetry Prize for his poem 'Sophie Robinson's Poetry'. He is a copywriter living in Tonbridge with his wife, Sophie, and an ever-changing quantity of animals. He studied Creative Writing at Greenwich University.

James Gaywood is an artist and writer. He has written for *Third Text* quarterly journal and his work was included in *Theory in Contemporary Art since 1985*, ed. Zoya Kocur and Simon Leung. His artwork includes natural themes, ideas of anthropocentricity and consciousness, but avoids participating in gallery-oriented displays, preferring to represent work in an immersive 'natural theatre'. For more contextualisation visit jamestheecreator.co.uk.

Chris Gutkind recently had poems from a sequence, 'Digits After Orph', in *Otoliths*, *Erotoplasty*, *Berfrois* and *Shearsman*. Other recent poems are in *Pamenar*. Books are *Inside to Outside* (Shearsman), *Options*, with artist Trevor Simmons (Knives Forks Spoons) and *What Happened* (unpublished). A photo project, *Isolation Collaboration*, is on Permeable Barrier and a short essay on *War and Peace* will be on the Pushkin House blog soon. 'Gravity Bubbles' appeared online at Babel Tower Notice Board previously though with a different design. Montreal. London. Librarian.

J L Hall's fiction, non-fiction and poetry is published in anthologies including *24 Stories*, *Tempest*, *A Narrative Map*, *AM Heath/TLC Reads*, *Rebel Alliance*, *Surfing*, *To Whom It May Concern*, *A Wild and Precious Life*, *The Mechanics' Institute Review* podcast and various places online. She has won and been finalist in several international and national writing prizes including the I Must Be Off! Travel Writing Competition, the Emerging Writer Award (The Bridge Awards) at Moniack Mhor, the Impress New Writers Prize and the Lucy Cavendish College Fiction Prize. J L Hall lives by the sea in Edinburgh where she teaches creative writing and works part-time as an academic.

Ziddy Ibn Sharam is a lost digital consciousness trapped in a rogue ethernet cable in Canary Wharf. Whilst trying to find a home, Ibn Sharam commenced hacking the servers of the City of London. In the process, Ibn Sharam authored the collections of poetry *Acharnement* (Distance No Object, 2021) and a series of Rubaiyat (forthcoming).

CONTRIBUTOR BIOGRAPHIES

Bryan Karetnyk is a British writer and translator. His translations include major works by Gaito Gazdanov, Irina Odoevtseva and Boris Poplavsky.

Daniel Kramb is a writer and poet. He is the author of three novels, *Central* (2015), *From Here* (2012) and *Dark Times* (2010); and a booklet of poetry, *Timid Takes* (2013). *Look at Us* is a play collaboration with JJ Bola. Daniel is a member of Malika's Poetry Kitchen and his prose history of the collective is forthcoming in their new anthology, *Too Young, Too Loud, Too Different*.

Dal Kular is a writer, poet, zine-maker and therapeutic creative writing facilitator living in Sheffield, UK. She is the curatrix of She Howls writing circles and open mics for women, running since 2018. She is currently working on an interdisciplinary memoir exploring grief, race, patriarchy and nature.

Eric Langley works in the English Department at UCL, where he lectures and writes on Shakespeare. His debut poetry collection, *Raking Light*, was published by Carcanet in 2017 and was shortlisted for the Felix Dennis Award for Best First Collection at that year's Forward Prizes. His poetry has appeared in *PN Review*, *Blackbox Manifold*, *3:AM Magazine* and *New Poetries VI* (Carcanet), and he has published pamphlets with Crater Press (with Emily Critchley) and Equipage.

Neha Maqsood is a Pakistani writer and journalist. Her poems have found a home in the *Kenyon Review*, *Ambit*, *Strange Horizons* and the *Aleph Review*. Her debut poetry book, *Vulnerability*, was awarded the Hellebore Poetry Scholarship Award and will be published by Hellebore Press in summer 2021. You can find her on Instagram @ItsNehaMaqsood.

Helen Marten is an artist based in London. Marten received The Turner Prize and Hepworth Prize for Sculpture, both 2016. In 2020, Marten published her first novel *The Boiled in Between*, with Prototype. Forthcoming solo exhibitions include Sadie Coles HQ, London; Greene Naftali, NYC; and The Garage Museum of Contemporary Art, Moscow.

Lila Matsumoto's publications include the poetry collection *Urn & Drum* (2018) and the chapbooks *Soft Troika* (2016) and *Allegories from my Kitchen* (2015). She plays in the band Food People and teaches poetry and creative-critical writing at the University of Nottingham. Her second full collection, *Two Twin Pipes Sprout Water*, is forthcoming from Prototype in November 2021. Her website is: lilamatsumoto.com.

Otis Mensah is a writer and performing artist with an alternative take on Hip-Hop music and abstract poetry. Focusing on art as a means of documenting journeys of introspection, Otis' work aims to demonstrate the personal and political power of vulnerable expression. Otis takes influence from the rhythmic and expressive freedom of Jazz and uses aesthetic language as an instrument to solo through themes of identity, existence and coming-of-age. His debut collection, *Safe Metamorphosis*, was published by Prototype in 2020.

Calliope Michail is a London-based poet & translator from Athens, Greece. She is the author of *Along Mosaic Roads* (2018), published with the87press. A leaflet of watercolour erasure poetry, *The Nature of the Physical Wor(l)d*, was printed in 2019 by Penteract Press with more poems from the project included in the press's *Science Poems* anthology. Other work has appeared in *Snow Lit Rev*, *Datableed*, *Pamenar Press*, *The Hythe* and more. www.calliopemichail.com

Lauren de Sá Naylor addresses embodiment in various states of consciousness/dualism-grappling. Her audio, visual & writing practice weaves collage-film, poetry, dream transcription, field recordings, voice and sound collage (released under the moniker LDSN). She received an MA in Critical Theory from the University of Leeds, lives & works in Todmorden, West Yorkshire, is 1/4 of an artist-run café-bar & is a parent.

Astra Papachristodoulou is a PhD researcher and tutor at the University of Surrey with a focus on experimental poetics. Her work has appeared in *The Times*, *Ambit* and *Magma Poetry*. She is the founder of Poem Atlas, an exhibition platform and publisher of visual poetry, and her work has been exhibited in a range of art venues including the National Poetry Library and the Poetry Café.

James Conor Patterson is from Newry in the north of Ireland. Recent poems and articles have appeared in *bath magg*, *The Irish Times*, *Poetry London*, *Poetry Ireland Review* and *The Poetry Review*, among others. In 2021 he was shortlisted for the White Review Poet's Prize and in 2019 he was a recipient of an Eric Gregory Award.

Oliver Sedano-Jones is a British-Peruvian writer. His work has appeared in *Banshee*, *Tears in the Fence*, *Ink Sweat and Tears* and *SPOONFEED*. He was shortlisted for the Yeats Prize in 2018, the University of Hertfordshire Single Poem Prize in 2019, and the Wales Poetry Award 2020.

Marcus Slease is a (mostly) absurdist, surrealist and minimalist writer from Portadown, N. Ireland and Utah. He is the author of *Never Mind the Beasts* (Dostoyevsky Wannabe), *The Green Monk* (Boiler House Press) and *Play Yr Kardz Right* (Dostoyevsky Wannabe), among others. Find out more on his website: www.nevermindthebeasts.com and follow him on Twitter: @postpran.

Maria Sledmere is editor-in-chief at SPAM Press and a member of A+E Collective. Recent publications include *Chlorophyllia* (OrangeApple Press), *neutral milky halo* (Guillemot Press), *varnish//cache* (If A Leaf Falls Press) and *Polychromatics* (Legitimate Snack). With Rhian Williams she co-edited the anthology *the weird folds: everyday poems from the anthropocene* (Dostoyevsky Wannabe). Current work includes a seasonal pamphlet series, *Sonnets for Hooch*, in collaboration with Mau Baiocco and Kyle Lovell. Her debut collection, *The Luna Erratum*, is forthcoming from Dostoyevsky Wannabe.

Andrew Spragg was born in London and lives there. Recent poetry books include *Now Too How Soon* (Contraband Books, 2017), *Dogtown* (Litmus, 2018, with the artist Beth Hopkins) and *O Buster* (Run Amok, 2021). *OoP*, a collection of otherwise out-of-print work, is forthcoming from Contraband Books this year. His work has appeared in *The Chicago Review*, *Datableed* and elsewhere. He has written critical pieces for *The Hythe*, *Hix Eros*, *The Quietus*, *Poetry London* and *PN Review*. A sporadic series of essays on radical tenderness can be found here: medium.com/@andrew.spragg84.

Nick Thurston is a writer and editor who makes artworks.

Olly Todd's poems have appeared in *Ambit*, *The Rialto*, *Vice*, *Test Centre*, *Five Dials* and the Clinic anthologies. His debut pamphlet *Odeum Spotlights* (Rough Trade Books, 2018), was long-listed for the Michael Marks Awards. He lives in London with his girlfriend and their daughter.

Nadia de Vries is a poet and critic from Amsterdam, the Netherlands. She is the author of *I Failed to Swoon* (2021) and *Dark Hour* (2018), both published by Dostoyevsky Wannabe, and also writes in Dutch. She holds a PhD in Cultural Analysis from the University of Amsterdam.

Stephen Watts' most recent books are *Ancient Sunlight* (Enitharmon, 2014 & 2020) & *Republic Of Dogs / Republic Of Birds* (Test Centre, 2016 & Prototype, 2020). A film, *The Republics*, based on the latter, was produced by Huw Wahl in 2019 & widely shown internationally. In 2021 he edited *Swirl Of Words / Swirl Of Worlds*, for an exhibition of the same name at PEER Gallery in Hoxton and his collaboration with the Swiss artist Hannes Schüpbach, *Explosion Of Words / Explosion Der Wörter*, was shown at the Strauhof in Zurich during June 2021 & is forthcoming at the Nunnery Gallery in Bow in early 2022. For this his monumental four-volume *Bibliography Of Modern Poetry In English Translation* was printed as an artist's book. In autumn 2022 Prototype will publish his *Collected Poems Vol. I : 1976–2005*. He feels that for some obscure reason luck has perhaps now turned its sun-marked gaze over in his direction, towards his being-in-many-places-at-once.

Karen Whiteson started out writing poetry, which has been published in numerous magazines and several anthologies. She subsequently became interested in narrative and so switched to prose fiction, favouring the short form. She has also written libretti for music theatre pieces performed at the ICA and The Riverside Studios. Her radio play *Tales for Louis* was broadcast on Radio 3 and her short stories have been published in the *Edinburgh Review* as well as in anthologies published by Penguin, Aurora Metro and Unthank Books. Her work can also be found online at *Ink Sweat & Tears* and *3:AM Magazine*. She has taught creative writing in a wide range of contexts including at The Poetry School, the Royal College of Art (Animation Dept.) and Central Saint Martins. She lives in London. She is currently working on a novel, from which 'Runaway Film' is excerpted.

Frances Whorrall-Campbell is an artist, writer and archivist. Their critical writing has appeared in *Art Monthly* and *Art-Agenda*, and their creative work has been published in anthologies by Pilot Press and Ugly Duckling Presse. They are the editor and curator of *Conversations Across Place*, an interdisciplinary workshop and publication promoting queer and decolonial approaches to landscape. Frances is currently a Research Associate at the Centre for Contemporary Art Derry~Londonderry.

Alice Willitts is a poet and plantswoman from the Fens. She is the author of *Think Thing: an ecopoetic practice* (Elephant

171

Press, 2020), *With Love* (Live Canon, 2020) and *Dear* (Magma, 2018). She is creator and editor of the ecopoetry collaboration series *DIRT*, forthcoming with Dialect in 2021, and was guest editor for *Magma 78: Collaborations* in 2020. She co-founded the biodiversity project On The Verge Cambridge. www.alicewillittspoet.uk

Frannie Wise is an illustrator, ceramicist and writer, recent graduate of the Edinburgh College of Art. She is a member of *The Student* newspaper and *Loaf* magazine and is also the graphic designer for social enterprise *The Noisy Movement*. Her work has been exhibited in Whitespace Gallery, Edinburgh, and The Queen's Hall, Hexham. Current works include cover designs for publishers such as *Great Star Communications*, Shanghai, and *AWW Magazine*, Hong Kong. She has designed the front cover of Anjeli Caderamanpulle's publication *Boys* (SPAM Press, 2020) and is an entrant of The Macmillan Prize 2021.

Antosh Wojcik is a poet, sound artist, drummer and member of the FWRDMTN creative house. His cross-disciplinary performance piece, *How To Keep Time: A Drum Solo for Dementia*, was commissioned by Penned in the Margins and toured the UK and internationally in 2019. He led the poetry and sound course 'Soundtext' for The Poetry School, 2020, prompting writers to fuse text and sound-making principles in their work. His writing has appeared in anthologies published by Bad Betty Press, Colliding Lines and Nine Arches Press.

ISBN 978-1-913513-19-1